When God Speaks

Henry Blackaby
Richard Blackaby

Everyday Discipleship Series

LifeWay Press
Nashville, Tennessee

ISBN 0-8054-9822-2

Dewey Decimal Classification: 231
Subject Heading: GOD // SPIRITUAL LIFE

This book is the text for course CG-0125 in the subject area Ministry
of the Christian Growth Study Plan.

Unless otherwise indicated, Scripture quotations are from *The Experiencing God Bible*,
copyright © 1994 by Broadman & Holman Publishers.
From the *New King James Version*. Copyright © 1979, 1980, 1982, Thomas Nelson, Inc., Publishers.

Order additional copies of this book by writing to Customer Service Center, MSN 113;
127 Ninth Avenue, North; Nashville, TN 37234-0113; by calling toll free (800) 458-2772;
by faxing (615) 251-5933; by ordering online at *www.lifeway.com*; by emailing
customerservice@lifeway.com; or by visiting a LifeWay Christian Store.

For information about adult discipleship and family resources, training, and events,
visit our Web site at *www.lifeway.com/discipleplus*.

Printed in the United States of America

LifeWay Press
127 Ninth Avenue, North
Nashville, Tennessee 37234

As God works through us, we will help people and churches know Jesus Christ
and seek His kingdom by providing biblical solutions that
spiritually transform individuals and cultures.

Contents

The Authors

Henry Blackaby has devoted his life to knowing and experiencing God. He grew up in the home of a Baptist deacon and lay church planter. He watched his godly parents faithfully serving the Lord in cities and towns across British Columbia, Canada, where there was often no evangelical witness.

Henry graduated from the University of British Columbia and earned his B.Div. and Th.M. from Golden Gate Baptist Theological Seminary. He was honored in 1992 by Hardin Simmons University with a D.D. Henry has served as pastor in three churches, including two in California and Faith Baptist Church in Saskatoon, Saskatchewan. He led the Capilano Baptist Association in Vancouver as its Director of Missions and now serves as a special consultant to the presidents of the Home and Foreign Mission Boards, and The Sunday School Board of the Southern Baptist Convention in the area of Prayer and Spiritual Awakening. Henry is a popular conference speaker and has authored several books including, *Experiencing God: Knowing and Doing the Will of God*; *Fresh Encounter: God's Pattern for Revival and Spiritual Awakening*; *Called and Accountable*; *What the Spirit is Saying to the Churches*; *Lift High the Torch!*, and was the general editor for *The Experiencing God Study Bible*.

Henry and his wife Marilynn have five children, all of whom have responded to God's call into full-time Christian ministry. Richard serves as president of the Canadian Southern Baptist Seminary; Thomas is associate pastor of Friendship Baptist Church in Winnipeg, Manitoba; Melvin serves as pastor to Hillcrest Baptist Church in Kamloops, British Columbia; and Norman and Carrie are students at Southwestern Baptist Theological Seminary. Henry and Marilynn are the proud grandparents of six grandchildren. They make their home in Rex, Georgia.

Richard Blackaby is the oldest child of Henry and Marilynn. He graduated from the University of Saskatchewan with a B.A. in history and earned an M.Div. and Ph.D. from Southwestern Baptist Theological Seminary. He and his wife Lisa have three children; Michael, Daniel, and Carrie.

Richard served as pastor of Friendship Baptist Church in Winnipeg, Manitoba, before accepting the position of President to the Canadian Southern Baptist Seminary in Cochrane, Alberta.

Introduction

In 1970, my wife Marilynn and I faced a major decision. I was the pastor of a wonderful church in California. One day I received a telephone call from Canada. A church of ten people in Saskatoon, Saskatchewan, wanted me to come as their pastor. They were discouraged and their church was about to dissolve.

On one hand, I saw that God had been richly blessing my church in California. People were responding to the gospel. I had four children, and their futures would be radically affected by a move to Canada. From a human perspective it seemed that there would be more opportunities to spread the gospel from a strong base in California than from the vast expanses of the Canadian prairies. I had friends travel great distances to discourage me from moving. They said I would never be heard of again by my denomination, and that I might not "survive" the bitterly cold Canadian winters! Faced with such a decision, I needed to know clearly what God had to say.

Marilynn and I came to believe that God was calling us to Canada, and we accepted His invitation. God richly blessed our subsequent ministry. Numerous mission churches were begun, and a theological training center was established. Most significantly for our family, all five of our children grew up in a mission setting where each one felt God's call to full-time Christian service. God has also been gracious to me and used my life in ways I never could have dreamed! I didn't perish in a snow storm! How tragic it would have been if I had misunderstood what God was saying to me!

In 1990 Claude King and I wrote *Experiencing God: Knowing and Doing the Will of God*. Over and over, people have said that it has helped them address their heartfelt need to know when God is speaking to them. As a result of the tremendous response to *Experiencing God*, my son Richard and I have written this course to give a more extensive treatment to the important truths concerning God's speaking to His people. This course is based on units five and six of *Experiencing God*.

What an honor to write a book with my eldest son! God is so good! God has let us see and experience His love and grace in wonderful ways. We have seen much together. Now, as adults, we see the unfolding of His purposes and ways in our lives and our families from unique perspectives. Richard has added much to this book, in illustrations and in subtle and significant ways. It has truly been a joint venture.

As Marilynn has been a wonderful helpmate to me as we wrote, Richard's wife Lisa added unique and valuable suggestions. Others, such as Connie Taillon, Karen Nault, Wayne and Andi Cook, Bill Falkner, Kerry Skinner, Andrea McGriff, and Lois Bradshaw graciously helped.

Our prayer is that this book will add something special to God's people, who so desperately desire to know when God is speaking to them. May God accomplish this as His people read and study His Word together!

About This Study

The purpose of this course is to assist you in knowing when God is speaking to you and what He is saying. My experience in walking with God has shown me that God does speak to His servants. He gives clear, personal instructions which enable you to experience fully His power, presence, and love. You will come to understand how God speaks to you by His Holy Spirit through the Bible, prayer, circumstances, and the church. As you study this course, you will be invited to share in a small-group setting what God says to you.

The format of this course is simple. The major ways in which God speaks to His people are covered in six weeks. In each week there are five lessons to be done individually. Only one lesson should be done per day. Each lesson should take 15 to 20 minutes, but when God speaks to you, you may want to continue responding to what He is saying. The purpose of this course is not that you gain more head knowledge but that you genuinely experience God speaking to you. Work on the materials as the Holy Spirit directs you.

There is a Scripture memory verse each week. Let these six passages become part of your mind and heart. If you are not experienced in Scripture memorization, the information below offers suggestions that others have found to be helpful.

1. Read the verse and think about the meaning.
2. Write the verse on note cards, one phrase per card.
3. Glance at the first phrase and say it aloud. Glance at the next phrase and say both phrases aloud. Continue this process until you have said the whole verse.
4. Try to say the verse form memory later in the day. If you cannot remember the complete verse, glance at the cards to refresh your memory.
5. Repeat the verse several times each day for a week or until you feel that the verse is firmly implanted in your mind.

At the end of each week is a question often asked about that week's subject. Prayerfully consider the answer and, if this is a question you might be asking, implement the answers in your daily walk.

Each daily lesson concludes with two questions: What did God say to you today? and What will you do as a result? Meditate on these questions and answer them honestly. They will serve as a journal during the six weeks. You will want to review them at the end of your study.

At the end of each week, gather with a group that is also studying the material. Share and discuss all God said to you during the week. Accept this responsibility or enlist a leader to facilitate your discussion. The leader's role is to help you to understand all that God is saying and to encourage you to respond to God's Word in obedience. A Leader Guide is provided in the back of the book.

GOD SPEAKS

MEMORY VERSE

"Man shall not live by bread alone; but man lives by every word that proceeds from the mouth of the LORD" (Deut. 8:3).

THIS WEEK'S LESSONS

Day 1: God Speaks to His People
Day 2: God Speaks Words of Life
Day 3: God Speaks in Various Ways
Day 4: God Speaks to Reveal Himself, His Purposes, and His Ways
Day 5: God Speaks and Requires a Response

SUMMARY OF WEEK 1

This week you will:
• identify at least two hindrances to hearing God's word;
• share how you have responded to God's word;
• list ways God spoke to people in the Bible;
• demonstrate ways God's purposes have been fulfilled in your life; and,
• identify the "soil type" of your heart.

GOD SPEAKS CONCERNING MISSIONS

I was in a meeting of national denominational prayer leaders. We were focusing on prayer and global evangelism. I shared how God had been working mightily through our missionaries to reach thousands of Massai tribesmen in southwest Kenya when for years there had been no response to the gospel.

After I had shared, a former missionary to Tanzania from another denomination, and now a denominational prayer leader, spoke with strong emotion. "While I was a missionary in Tanzania, I traveled a road in the northwest of the country where I saw the Massai. I knew they had never responded to the gospel. God told me to pray for them and that one day they would respond. For 12 years I prayed for their salvation as I traveled those roads. While I served there, I never saw them accept the gospel. Now I have heard that God is using your missionaries to reach them for Christ and I rejoice greatly!"

I felt a deep sense of humility. God may have used our missionaries to complete what He had told this dear woman He would do many years ago. She had believed the word God gave her about the Massai and God had faithfully kept His word to her. When God speaks, we are to obey, even if we do not see the results ourselves or are not used by God to be a part of His answer to our prayer. God will see that His word to us comes to pass.

Day 1

GOD SPEAKS TO HIS PEOPLE

There are few truths in Scripture more exciting than this: God speaks to His people. The same God who created the universe with a word, now speaks to us. There are at least two things that prevent people from having God's word radically transform their lives.

First is sin. Sin disorients us to God and causes us to stop seeking Him. Read Romans 3:11. Sin makes us self-centered instead of God-centered. Sin causes our prayers to go unheard and quenches the Spirit's working within us.

Second, worldly things dull our senses to receiving a word from God. For example, the average household spends over seven hours with their television on each day! When you watch television you do so to gain information or for entertainment. Too often our thinking becomes blurred. One moment we are watching a dramatic reenactment of a battle scene depicting suffering and death, and then with the push of a button we can see a war-torn country where real people are suffering and dying. Our hearts have already been numbed to death and dying. So, we walk away from our television unmoved and unchanged.

We can approach God's word in the same way. God's word is never for our entertainment, information, or observation, but obedience. God's word never allows us to remain the same. Today, many Christians are uncertain when God is speaking to them.

 Describe two hindrances to hearing a word from God.

1. _____

2. _____

> "There is none who understand; There is none who seeks after God" (Rom. 3:11).

All of our understanding must be taken from Scripture. Too many people base their Christianity on human reasoning. It is easy to assume that God relates to you in the same way that people relate to each other. This is untrue. You may need to make adjustments in your life to experience fully God speaking to you. Whenever my experience does not match what I find revealed in Scripture, I immediately seek to bring my experience into conformity with Scripture and not the other way around.

God speaks throughout the Bible. Genesis 1 repeatedly states, "God spoke … it was so … it was good." What God says *always* comes to pass and it is always good. Read Isaiah 14:24,27.

> "The Lord of hosts has sworn, saying, 'Surely, as I have thought, so it shall come to pass, And as I have purposed, so it shall stand. … For the LORD of hosts has purposed, And who will annul it? His hand is stretched out, And who will turn it back?' " (Isa. 4:24,27).

GOD'S PATTERN

There are several characteristics of the way God spoke to people in the Bible.

❑ Though God used many ways to speak to His people, the key is *that* God spoke, not *how* He spoke. Those to whom God spoke focused on God's message, not the means by which He spoke.

❑ Whenever God spoke, the person knew it was God. Scripture indicates we *will* know God's voice.

❑ When God spoke, the person knew what God said. Usually our problem is not in knowing what God says, but in our willingness to obey what we know He is saying to us.

❑ When God spoke, the person knew what to do in response and could no longer carry on "business as usual." The issue was a matter of obedience.

❑ The person who received a word from God could not always prove to others that God had spoken. He could only obey and allow the results to testify to God's work.

 Think about a time in your life when God spoke to you. Place a check by each characteristic above that was evident in your encounter with God. Was obedience an issue? Why or why not?

_____

_____

GOD'S WORD CAME TO PASS!

As a pastor in Saskatoon, God impressed on my heart that He wanted me to be a catalyst for revival and spiritual awakening across North America. He also showed me that an important element to God's doing this in Canada was by raising up and training leaders. I responded to all God said to me. I studied the great awakenings and prayed with fellow pastors. We began a Bible college to equip people for Christian leadership. Many received training and strengthened churches across Canada. While in Saskatoon, I was privileged to participate in a revival that took place in the early 1970s.

Then God called me to serve as a Director of Missions in Vancouver. The school I had helped to found was closed. There were no city-wide revivals in Vancouver. I had to trust that the word God had given me concerning spiritual awakening and theological education would come to pass.

God has been so faithful in fulfilling His word to me! In November 1993, I had the privilege of preaching the installation sermon for my oldest son, Richard, as he was inducted as the president of our new seminary in Canada. God's word concerning spiritual awakening has also not returned "void." I was invited to serve as a special consultant to the presidents of our Home, Foreign, and Sunday School boards in the area of Prayer and Spiritual Awakening. What God says will come to pass and it is always good!

Knowing when God is speaking to you is not difficult! Like all forms of communication, your relationship with God needs to be cultivated.

What did God say to you during your study today?

_____

_____

What will you do as a result?

_____

_____

Day 2

GOD SPEAKS WORDS OF LIFE

"Man shall not live by bread alone; but man lives by every word that proceeds from the mouth of the LORD" (Deut. 8:3).

"Set your hearts on all the words which I testify among you today, which you shall command your children to be careful to observe—all the words of this law. For it is not a futile thing for you, because it is your life" (Deut. 32:46-47).

God does not speak to us merely so we can have a warm, devotional thought. God's words are essential to our lives. Focus on Deuteronomy 8:3, this week's memory verse. Write it on a card and put it in a prominent place. Deuteronomy 32:46-47 tells us how important a word from God is. Read it and reflect on what it means in your life.

How important is a word from God for your life? Check one.
❑ very important   ❑ important   ❑ not very important

Read Luke 7:14-15 on page 11. What significance did God's words have for the widow's dead son? Underline your answer in the verses.

Read Ezekiel 37:5-6,10 on page 11. What effect did God's words have on a valley of dry bones when the prophet Ezekiel was told to preach to them? Underline your answer in the verses.

God's words bring life! God's word never leaves someone or something the same. However, many Christians have lost the sense of awe at receiving a word from God. We no longer stand before God with fear and trembling, waiting to hear His word for our life. Can you imagine? The same word that can create a solar system or raise the dead can be directed to speak about our lives and God's plans for us! How that ought to make us tremble!

I am concerned when Christians trivialize God's Word. God's Word is far too important for us not to take it seriously. There is too much at stake for us to be careless with a word from God. God has clear guidelines and they need to be known and followed.

I am also concerned that many Christians feel awkward about acknowledging that God spoke to them. We fear we will sound too spiritual or mystical in spite of the fact that the Bible is full of examples of God speaking to people. We should encourage each other to testify to what we are hearing from God.

SHARING GOD'S WORD CAN MAKE A DIFFERENCE

Connie had returned to her home church after spending several years away in missions. As a young girl was presented to the church for baptism at the close of a service, Connie noticed something that troubled her deeply. To Connie's dismay, few people took the time to go by the front of the church and encourage the young girl. This was very unlike what this church had done in the past. She went home that afternoon and the Holy Spirit impressed upon her that what she had witnessed was wrong. That evening, at the prompting of the interim pastor, she shared with the church what she sensed God was saying. Instantly the Spirit confirmed in the hearts of the people that what was being shared was of God. The people's eyes were opened to how careless they had become in acknowledging decisions in their church. Many people made new commitments which have lasted to this day.

 How do you respond to God when He speaks through members of your church?

_____

Does God want you to change the way you respond when He speaks to you through others? ❏ Yes ❏ No **What change does God desire?**

_____

_____

"Then He came and touched the open coffin, and those who carried him stood still. And He said, "Young man, I say to you, arise." And he who was dead sat up and began to speak. And He presented him to his mother" (Luke 7:14-15).

" 'Thus says the Lord God to these bones: "Surely I will cause breath to enter into you, and you shall live. I will put sinews on you and bring flesh upon you, cover you with skin and put breath into you; and you shall live. Then you shall know that I am the Lord." 'So I prophesied as He commanded me, and breath came into them, and they lived, and stood upon their feet, an exceedingly great army" (Ezek. 37:5-6,10).

How are you sharing with others what God is saying to you?

_____

_____

Churches can rob themselves of wonderful opportunities for God to speak to them by not encouraging their people to share what God is saying. There needs to be discernment and guidance concerning who shares and when, but even the largest churches should encourage their people to testify. This can be done in smaller group settings such as in a Bible study, a prayer group, or Sunday School class. I found the ordinance of baptism was a wonderful opportunity for people to testify to the life-transforming work of God in their lives. They did not always know the proper Christian terminology, but the Holy Spirit used their testimonies to impact the church. The enthusiasm of a new believer often warmed the hearts of those whose hearts had grown cold.

A word of caution: Although we ought to feel free to share with others what God said to us, we must be careful we do not claim to have had a word from God unless we do. It is a terrible thing for us to give credit to God for something that has not come from Him. Do not speak a word from God unless you are certain that it is from God and that you are willing to "stay with that word" until it comes to pass.

What did God say to you during your study today?

_____

_____

What will you do as a result?

_____

_____

Day 3

GOD SPEAKS IN VARIOUS WAYS

Even the most casual reading of Scripture reveals that throughout the ages, God has used a wide variety of means to speak.

 From the following list, check those that God used to speak to people in the Bible.

❏ dreams	❏ angels	❏ fleece
❏ prophets	❏ a trumpet	❏ preaching
❏ a donkey	❏ fire	

Did you check them all? God spoke to people in the Bible through …

- angels (Luke 1:26)
- visions (Gen. 15:1)
- dreams (Matt. 2:12-13)
- prophets (Acts 21:10-11)
- symbolic actions (Jer. 18:1-10)
- preaching (Jonah 3:4)
- a still small voice (1 Kings 19:12)
- miraculous signs (Ex. 8:20-25)
- a burning bush (Ex. 3:2)
- a donkey (Num. 22:28)
- prayer (Acts 22:17-18)
- a trumpet (Ex. 19:16, 19)
- fire (1 Kings 18:37-39)
- fleece (Judg. 6:36ff)
- writing on the wall (Dan. 5:5)
- casting lots (Acts 1:23-26)

Make a list of ways you know God speaks today.

- _____
- _____

- _____
- _____

God spoke "at various times" (Heb. 1:1). God did not speak at just one time of the day or one day of the week. He spoke to men in their youth and their old age. He spoke to people in the workplace—not only at church.

God speaks at various times in our lives. A growing number of senior adults are hearing a fresh word from God. To their surprise, God continues to speak to them about new assignments and many are responding with great joy! Many children and youth are experiencing a fresh word from God as well.

I do two things to be open to anything God wants to say to me …

1. I make myself accessible to many opportunities for God to communicate with me. For example, although God uses my quiet times with

Him to speak to me, He can and will also use the preaching of His Word at my church, a Bible study, or a Friday morning group prayer time. Quality conferences, reading books by particular Christian authors, or exercising certain Christian disciplines can also become ways to hear from God. Being a part of a local church is also important because it provides many opportunities and people through whom God can speak. Be careful that you do not limit God to just one way of speaking to you.

Jesus used a variety of times, places, and ways to speak to His disciples. Turn to Mark 1 in your Bible, and let's walk through this chapter, identifying times, places, and ways Jesus spoke.

1:14— "Jesus came to _____, _____ the gospel of the kingdom of God."

1:16— "And as he walked by the _____ of _____, He saw Simon and Andrew…"

1:21— "Then they went into _____, and immediately on the _____ He entered the_____ and _____."

1:29— "Now as soon as they had come out of the synagogue, they entered the _____ of Simon and Andrew."

1:32— "Now at _____, when the sun had set, they brought to Him all who were _____ and those who were _____."

1:35— "Now in the _____, having risen a long while _____ _____, He went out and departed to a _____ _____; and there He _____."

1:39— "And He was _____ in their _____ throughout all _____; and _____ out demons."

Throughout the Gospels, Jesus spoke at different times: in the morning and throughout the day, in the middle of the night, on the Sabbath, in the middle of the workweek; at meal times, during funerals, and in storms. He spoke at various places: on the mountainside, in the middle of an urban crowd, at parties, in the synagogue, in a boat, while walking along the road, in homes and in the temple. Jesus spoke in various ways: sermons, individual contacts, miracles, His personal example, the forces of nature, and the presence of children.

Check which of these ways you have heard God speaking to you.

❏ worship services	❏ Sunday School	❏ Bible study
❏ Christian books	❏ prayer	❏ music
❏ small-group studies	❏ work	❏ nature
❏ Christian films	❏ meditation	❏ fasting
❏ Christian conferences	❏ friends	❏ tapes
❏ walking	❏ spouse	❏ tragedy
❏ blessings	❏ world events	❏ mission speakers
❏ parents	❏ other _____	

If you are experiencing God speaking through only one or two methods, pray now and ask God if He wants to speak in other ways as well.

2. I cultivate my relationship with Christ. The more I know Him, the easier it is for me to recognize His voice. When I married Marilynn, I thought I knew her well. I soon discovered there was much I did not know. There were times I assumed I understood what she was telling me, only to discover to my disappointment that I had not. However, the more time I spent with her, the more I came to understand how she thought, what was important to her, and what she wanted to do. I came to anticipate things she would say or ways she would feel. Today, we can communicate a great deal and say very little. Catching my eye from across a room, giving me that certain look, or mentioning a person's name can tell an entire story! The more I know Marilynn and share experiences with her, the easier it is for us to communicate.

Our relationship to Christ is similar. When we first become Christians there is much about God we do not know and have not experienced. The longer and more intimately we relate to God, however, the more we come to know His presence and activity in our life. We build a history of shared experiences upon which we can draw to understand what God says to us.

Abraham is described as a friend of God (read Isa. 41:8). The Lord spoke to Moses as a friend (read Ex. 33:11a). Jesus called His disciples His friends (read John 15:15).

 Is your relationship with God intimate enough to describe God as your friend? ❏ Yes ❏ No How do you express your friendship with God?

_____

" 'But you, Israel, are My servant, Jacob, whom I have chosen, The descendants of Abraham My friend' " (Isa. 41:8).

"So the Lord spoke to Moses face to face, as a man speaks to his friend" (Ex. 33:11).

" 'No longer do I call you servants, for a servant does not know what his master is doing; but I have called you friends, for all things that I heard from My Father I have made known to you' " (John 15:15).

Is your relationship to God close enough that He would call you His friend? ❏ Yes ❏ No **On what do you base your answer?**

_____

_____

Don't be discouraged when Christians who are mature in the faith seem to have an easier time than you understanding how God is leading them. The longer we relate to God, the more we are "tuned in" to His voice and His communication with us. God constantly encourages His people to seek to know Him.

What did God say to you during your study today?

_____

_____

What will you do as a result?

_____

_____

Day 4

GOD SPEAKS TO REVEAL HIMSELF, HIS PURPOSES, AND HIS WAYS

As you begin today's study, write this week's memory verse in the margin above.

God always speaks with a purpose. No idle words come from our Lord's mouth. If we were to generalize the kinds of things God speaks about, we could say that God speaks in order to reveal Himself, His purposes, and His ways.

GOD SPEAKS TO REVEAL HIMSELF

Perhaps the most significant times that God speaks to you are when He wants you to understand a new dimension of who He is. You will never live a holy life without first understanding that you serve a holy God. You will never attempt the impossible until you believe that the God who commands you to do so is an all-powerful God. You will never be able to forgive others genuinely until you understand the incredible price God was willing to pay to forgive you. All of your activity with God is based on your understanding of who He is.

An important principle in God's dealing with us is that God reveals Himself to us progressively. Read Exodus 6:2-3. God revealed aspects of His character to Moses that He never shared with Abraham, Isaac, or Jacob. God's name of *Lord* was a window into the character and nature of God that had not been revealed previously. Jesus indicated there was much that God wanted to reveal to the disciples, but He would not disclose more than they could handle. If God is not revealing deep truths to you, it is not that He does not want to, but that you are not yet capable of responding to more than God has already shown you. Only time and experience with God will bring you to a mature relationship with Him.

"God spoke to Moses and said to him: 'I am the Lord. I appeared to Abraham, to Isaac, and to Jacob, as God Almighty, but by My name LORD I was not known to them' " (Ex. 6:2-3).

 What has God revealed to you about Himself lately?

_____

_____

GOD SPEAKS TO REVEAL HIS PURPOSES

When God speaks to His people, God reveals His heart. God is on mission to redeem a lost world. God expects people to adjust their lives to Him so that He can work through them to bring others to Himself.

Consider some of the purposes of God. Underline key words and phrases in the following verses that tell of God's purposes.

> "For I know the thoughts that I think toward you, says the LORD, thoughts of peace and not of evil, to give you a future and a hope" (Jer. 29:11).

> " 'Call to Me, and I will answer you, and show you great and mighty things, which you do not know' " (Jer. 33:3).

> "For the Son of Man has come to seek and to save that which was lost" (Luke 19:10).

FOR FURTHER STUDY
Read John 4:1-42 and see what difference knowing who Jesus was made in the life of the woman at the well. (Note especially verse 10). Write a brief summary in the space below.

 From these verses, what do we know about the purposes of God?

_____

_____

What God purposes, He brings to pass. It is God's purpose to bring His children into conformity with His Son. God's purposes are extremely different from ours. Our purpose in a situation may be to "do" something great for God, while God's purpose might be to build our character. At times we do not hear a word from God because we want Him to speak to us about *our* plans and purposes. Instead, God says, "I have no interest in speaking about how I can help your purposes, I want to talk about how you can adjust your life so that I can use you to accomplish Mine."

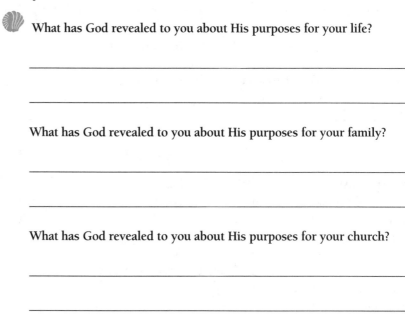

What has God revealed to you about His purposes for your life?

_____

_____

What has God revealed to you about His purposes for your family?

_____

_____

What has God revealed to you about His purposes for your church?

_____

_____

" 'For My thoughts are not your thoughts, Nor are your ways My ways,' says the Lord. 'For as the heavens are higher than the earth, So are My ways higher than your ways, And My thoughts than your thoughts' " (Isa. 55:8-9).

"Show me Your ways, O LORD; Teach me Your paths. Who is the man that fears the LORD? Him shall He teach in the way He chooses" (Ps. 25:4,12).

GOD SPEAKS TO REVEAL HIS WAYS

God's ways are not our ways. Read Isaiah 55:8-9. David understood that his ways were not God's ways. Read Psalm 25:4,12. A fundamental problem with many Christians and churches is that they do not realize that God does things in radically different ways than people do.

Oftentimes the way God acts is more important than what He does. Some Christians have assumed that the end justifies the means. Yet, the *way* we do something can say more about what we believe about God than *what* we do. We can completely disgrace the cause of Christ at the very time we are doing something for Him because we do it in a way that is not sanctioned by a holy God. Fighting a religious war or deceiving someone to get them to attend your church might be examples of doing things the wrong way. "For the ways of man are before the eyes of the LORD" (Prov. 5:21).

Psalm 103:7 makes an interesting distinction: "He made known His ways to Moses, His acts to the children of Israel." God said the children of Israel saw the *acts* of God as He performed miracles to deliver them, but Moses came to understand the *way* God worked. Are you satisfied with only seeing the end result of God's activity and never coming to know God through the *way* He acts?

When God's ways are followed by an individual, a family, or a church, fear and reverence may come upon those around them as they realize that there is something divine about what is being done. This was experienced by the entire church when Annanias and Saphira did not follow God's ways. "Great fear came upon all the church and upon all who heard these things" (Acts 5:11).

Do people fear the God of your church? Your denomination? If not, could it be because the way you are doing things is no different from the ways of the world? Many churches are just like the world around them. The people in the church see nothing to cause them to recognize the presence and power of God.

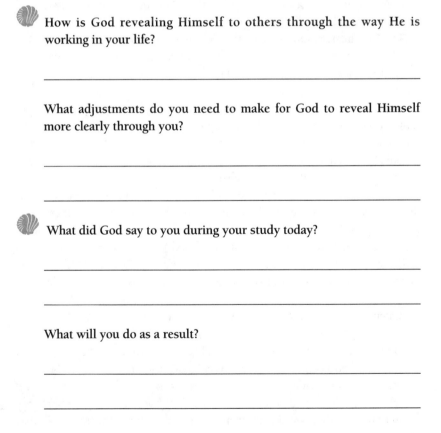

How is God revealing Himself to others through the way He is working in your life?

_____

_____

What adjustments do you need to make for God to reveal Himself more clearly through you?

_____

_____

_____

What did God say to you during your study today?

_____

_____

_____

What will you do as a result?

_____

_____

_____

FOR FURTHER STUDY
Read 2 Samuel 6:1-11. How did God deal with His people when they attempted to do something in a way He had not prescribed? Write your answer in the space below.

Day 5

GOD SPEAKS AND REQUIRES A RESPONSE

FOR FURTHER STUDY
Study Luke 6:46-49.
Identify two different
responses to receiving a
word from God. Write them
in the space below.

People will say, "You talk as if God speaks to you all the time, but that has not been my experience. I never hear God speaking to me!" Our understanding of God and how He works should never be based on our experience. How arrogant of us to assume that our experience is the measure of how God functions in our world. Rather, we always take our experience to the Word of God and then bring our experience into conformity with what God reveals.

Luke 8:5-15 explains how the condition of your heart can determine your response to God's word. Jesus described a sower who was casting seeds upon the earth. These seeds represented God's word coming to people's lives. According to Jesus there were four ways people responded to this word. Jesus said the way you respond to the word of God reveals the condition of your heart, and will determine what God will do in your life.

The first heart response: seed that fell by the wayside. Here is a path well traveled. As soon as the word comes, "the devil comes and takes away the word out of their hearts, lest they should believe and be saved" (v. 12). The soil of their heart is so hardened that a word from God cannot penetrate it. What is the condition of your heart? Are you allowing the world constantly to pass over your heart through the television and movies you watch, the music you listen to, the books you read, and the thoughts you have? When you allow your heart to become hardened and desensitized by the things of the world, God's word does not penetrate your heart in order to change your life.

The second heart response: seed falling on rocky, shallow ground. At first there is a joyful response but then, because the soil is shallow and there is no root, the person "falls away." We can attend a church service and even be an active participant, yet never let the word of God penetrate our lives. The word enters our minds but not our hearts. "Why do you call Me 'Lord, Lord,' and not do the things which I say?" (Luke 6:46). This is one reason we must meditate on God's Word.

The third heart response: seed which fell on thorny ground. These people hear the word from God but the cares, riches, and pleasures of life are so important to them that God's word is choked out. I cannot tell you how many times I have had people come to me weeping after a service. They sensed God calling them to Christian ministry or missions, but they first wanted to get married. Then their children came and their first house mortgage. Before they knew it, years had passed. Rather than responding to the word from God, they found themselves caught in the middle of the rat race of daily life. Years later they realized that their precious word from God had been choked out and had never borne fruit as God had purposed.

Jesus indicated that the first three heart conditions produced no fruit. It was not that their busyness and preoccupation or careless handling of God's word caused them to produce only a little fruit. In Jesus' eyes there was no fruit worthy of mention.

The fourth heart response: seed that fell on good ground and produced a great harvest! I have desired in my life always to have a heart so open and unobstructed that any word coming to me from God can multiply in me as God desires. That is why I regularly take inventory of the soil of my life. I often ask, Have any obstacles or sins entered my life? Am I letting the world trample my heart so that it is insensitive to a word from God? Am I trying to juggle a word from God along with all my worldly cares and concerns? Am I quick not only to hear a word, but joyfully to take action and obey?

 What type of soil is your heart providing to receive a word from God? Circle the number of the statement that best describes your heart.

1. Trampled, hardened soil (a heart hardened by too much traffic)
2. Rocky, shallow soil (entering the mind but not the heart)
3. Thorny soil full of weeds (a life too cluttered with worldliness to sustain a word from God)
4. Fertile, receptive soil (a heart open to hear and obey)

If you have not received a fresh word from God lately, return to the last word you were given, and see what you did in response. God may be refusing to give you a new word until you properly respond to the last word He gave.

 What is the last thing you know God clearly said to you?

_____

_____

What have you done with that word?

_____

_____

Based on how you responded to God's last word to you, are you ready for a new word from God? ❑ Yes ❑ No   Why or why not?

_____

_____

What did God say to you during your study this week?

_____

_____

What will you do as a result?

_____

_____

"For we do not wrestle against flesh and blood, but against principalities, against powers, against the rulers of the darkness of this age, against spiritual hosts of wickedness in the heavenly places" (Eph. 6:12).

" 'My sheep hear My voice, and I know them, and they follow Me' " (John 10:27).

A QUESTION COMMONLY ASKED

How can I know that God is speaking to lead me instead of Satan trying to mislead me? Remember that Satan is not the "evil equivalent" of God. Satan is only a creature who was created by God and who is entirely under subjection to God (see Rom. 16:20; Rev. 20:7). Satan is not omnipresent; He can only be in one place at one time (see Job 1:6-7).

Satan does have other spiritual forces that *do* wage war against us (read Eph. 6:12). However, those who belong to Jesus hear His voice and follow Him (read John 10:27). When a false shepherd comes, the sheep will not follow because they do not recognize his voice. We should strive to know God's voice so intimately that we immediately recognize other voices as not being from God. We can protect ourselves further by understanding that God will never lead us in a way that contradicts His Word. God is consistent in the way He leads.

Week 2

GOD SPEAKS BY THE HOLY SPIRIT

MEMORY VERSE

"However, when He, the Spirit of truth, has come, He will guide you into all truth; for He will not speak on His own authority, but whatever He hears He will speak; and He will tell you things to come" (John 16:13).

THIS WEEK'S LESSONS

Day 1: Be Enabled by the Spirit
Day 2: Be Acquainted with the Spirit's Work
Day 3: Be Filled with the Spirit
Day 4: Be Led by the Spirit
Day 5: Be Obedient to the Spirit

SUMMARY OF WEEK 2

This week you will:
• describe the enabling work of the Spirit of God;
• identify the names describing the work of the Holy Spirit;
• relate to your life the four steps of being Spirit-filled;
• identify the fruit of the Spirit in your life; and,
• examine your obedience to the Spirit.

THE HOLY SPIRIT ALERTED US TO PRAY

Many are the testimonies of the mighty workings of the Holy Spirit in people's lives. On one occasion the Spirit alerted Marilynn to awaken me and plead with me to join her in prayer for our three sons who were returning on icy roads from a student retreat 350 miles away. We knelt and prayed. Peace came. Later, our children told us how suddenly their car hit a sheet of black ice and spun out of control down the middle of the undivided highway at 60 miles per hour. Only five seconds before, their car had met a large truck. If that truck had passed five seconds later, everyone in the car most likely would have been killed. We determined that the accident was exactly at the time we had been alerted to pray for them! Our immediate, obedient response to what God says to us can be critical!

$\mathscr{D}ay$ *1*

BE ENABLED BY THE SPIRIT

"God is Spirit, and those who worship Him must worship in spirit and truth" (John 4:24).

It is critical that we know how to relate to the Spirit of God. Only those who lived in Jesus' day had the privilege of looking upon God in the flesh. For most of history, however, God has related to man by His Spirit.

Throughout the Old Testament, whenever God gave a direction to His people, He would place His Spirit upon them and enable them to perform His assignment. God's assignment was always God-sized and impossible to accomplish without divine intervention. God placed His Spirit on Moses and those who led with him in order to guide the Israelites through the wilderness for 40 years (see Num. 11:17). Each of the judges of the Israelites judged Israel with the enabling presence of the Spirit of God. The Spirit of God came upon Gideon and empowered him and his army to know how to defeat miraculously the Midianites who were oppressing God's people (Judg. 6:34). When David was anointed to be the next king of Israel, the Spirit of God was with him "from that day forward" (1 Sam. 16:13). The Spirit of God worked through each of the Old Testament prophets who spoke on behalf of the Lord (2 Pet. 1:21). In each case, the Spirit of the Lord guided and instructed men and women to accomplish things that would have been impossible apart from divine assistance.

When Jesus began His public ministry, the Spirit descended upon Him like a dove (Luke 3:22). The Spirit led Jesus into the wilderness to be tempted (Luke 4:1). Isaiah foretold that the Spirit of God would rest upon the Messiah (Isa. 11:2; Luke 4:18). Jesus was dependent upon the Spirit of God for His ministry. "The words that I speak to you I do not speak on My own authority; but the Father who dwells in Me does the works" (John 14:10).

As Jesus prepared His disciples for His departure, He told them what the role of the Holy Spirit would be. Just as Jesus had been dependent upon the working and guiding of the Spirit of God in His life, so the disciples depended entirely upon Jesus for their instruction and guidance. Now that He was leaving, Jesus said He would pray and ask the Father to send another Helper to come and remain with them forever (John 14:16). The Spirit would come from the Father and bear witness of Christ (John 15:26). He would not speak on His own authority even as Jesus had not. "Whatever He hears He will speak" (John 16:13). The Spirit of God would be present in the throne room of God and whatever He heard He would share with believers! (1 Cor. 2:9-12).

Jesus told His disciples not to go anywhere until they had received the Holy Spirit. "Behold, I send the Promise of My Father upon you; but tarry in the city of Jerusalem until your are endued with power from on high" (Luke 24:49).

Once the Spirit came upon them, they would have all the resources necessary to carry out any assignment (Acts 1:8). Acts 2 tells how the Spirit came upon the disciples and, where they once were timid witnesses, now they had boldness. Whereas they had not understood the most basic Scriptures before, now Peter could explain Scripture so that 3,000 people were added to the church (see Acts 2:5-47).

 What kinds of things did the Spirit of God enable people to do? Go back and underline words in the previous paragraphs that describe the activity of God's Spirit.

What kinds of things has the Spirit of God guided and enabled *you* to do in the past? What could He enable you to do in the future?

Past: _____

Future: _____

The Spirit of God enabled people to do things that were impossible apart from His help. He guided them to lead the people of God; to defeat enemies; to construct a tabernacle; to prophesy; to understand truth; to preach boldly; to understand Scripture and many other things. God's Spirit can lead you to do anything He assigns you to do.

 What did the Spirit say to you during your study today?

_____

_____

How will you respond to Him?

_____

_____

" 'However, when He, the Spirit of truth, has come, He will guide you into all truth; for He will not speak on His own authority, but whatever He hears He will speak; and He will tell you things to come' " (John 16:13). Write out on a card John 16:13, your memory verse this week. Put it in a prominent place so you can review it.

Day 2

BE ACQUAINTED WITH THE SPIRIT'S WORK

God speaks by His Holy Spirit. The names of the Holy Spirit help us understand how crucial He is in our lives if we are to know when God is speaking to us. A Hebrew person's name indicated character. Several names given to the Spirit reveal the ways in which God the Father purposes to speak to us by His Spirit.

HELPER

"And I will pray the Father, and He will give you another Helper, that He may abide with you forever–" (John 14:16)

"You shall receive power when the Holy Spirit has come upon you" (Acts 1:8).

Read John 14:16. Jesus prepared His disciples for His departure by telling them that the Father would send *another Helper* to them. The word *another* indicated that the helper would be of the exact same nature and character of Jesus. Throughout Scripture God revealed Himself as a "help" to His people. For example, when the Israelites were trapped between the Red Sea and the murderous Egyptian army, God's help was decisive.

In Acts, a new era began for the people of God. The Holy Spirit was to help the people in every way the Father and Son had. He would be just as practical and powerful in the way He guided God's people (read Acts 1:8).

 Is there anything God has spoken to you that you have been reluctant to do because you felt inadequate? If so, approach God, admit your weakness, and ask for His strength as you obey Him.

TEACHER

One of the most common titles used for Jesus in the Gospels was "Rabbi" or, "Teacher." In Jesus' day, there were no school buildings. Instead, the disciples lived with Jesus and went wherever He went. Each day they sat at His feet and listened to His teachings. Many times the teachings came directly out of the experiences they shared. Jesus' disciples listened to Him teach from a fishing boat as well as from a mountain top. They experienced teaching by example when Jesus washed their feet. Jesus reminded them that the Holy Spirit would be their Teacher and Guide.

I remind people who attend conferences where I speak that I am not the teacher. The Holy Spirit is their teacher, and He is present. People respond in different ways to the same message. Although everyone hears the same words audibly, the Holy Spirit personalizes each message to teach each individual the lesson he or she needs to learn at that moment. Your pastor, Sunday School teacher, or well-meaning Christian friend is the means the Spirit uses to teach you, but only the Holy Spirit can teach you spiritual truth.

In the margin, draw a symbol (stick figures are fine) or write a phrase that describes a spiritual truth that the Spirit has taught you recently.

REMINDER

Unfortunately, Christians tend to forget what their Teacher said. In the midst of circumstances, the Spirit will remind you of what God said to you previously (read John 14:26). For a missionary couple in a difficult situation, the Spirit may remind them of the time God called them into missions. To the person struggling with a decision, the Spirit may bring to mind a Scripture that speaks directly to his situation. Do not take for granted those times when your mind remembers a passage of Scripture or a word God spoke to you. This may be the activity of the Holy Spirit reminding you of what God has said already.

"But the Helper, the Holy Spirit … will … bring to your remembrance all things that I said to you" (John 14:26).

 What Scripture does the Holy Spirit bring to your mind? Write it below. What is God telling you through this Scripture?

_____

_____

SPIRIT OF TRUTH

Jesus described the Holy Spirit as the "Spirit of truth" (read John 14:17). Just as Jesus was the "way, the truth, and the life" (John 14:6), so now the Spirit is your infallible Guide to God's truth for your life. When Jesus stood at the tomb of Lazarus, only He knew the truth of that situation. Mary and Martha's perspective of their circumstances was: "Lord, if You had been here, my brother would not have died" (John 11:32). In John 11 we find a devastating representation of what our lives are like without the Spirit of truth. From a human perspective, a situation can seem hopeless. I believe that is why Jesus wept. He was grieved to see how hopelessly His friends faced death, when *He* knew there was hope and victory even in the face of life's greatest challenge. Jesus knew that Lazarus would soon be leaving the tomb. You do not know the truth of a situation until you have heard from the Spirit of truth.

"even the Spirit of truth, whom the world cannot receive, because it neither sees Him nor knows Him; but you know Him, for He dwells with you and will be in you" (John 14:17).

Jesus was the perfect counselor (read John 2:24-25). The Holy Spirit is the perfect counselor. There is no one who can more effectively address the deep needs of your life than the Spirit of God. The Spirit will not always tell you what you want to hear, but He will tell you the truth concerning your life and church.

"But Jesus did not commit Himself to them, because He knew all men, had no need that anyone should testify of man, for He knew what was in man" (John 2:24-25).

Has the Spirit of truth led you to do or believe something that you only came to fully understand later? ❑ Yes ❑ No What was it?

_____

_____

SPIRIT OF CONVICTION

" 'No one can come to Me unless the Father who sent Me draws him; and I will raise him up at the last day' " (John 6:44).

Those of us who know that Jesus is Lord are fully persuaded that only the Spirit of God could guide us to such a conviction. There are times we all need to be reminded that only the Spirit can convict people (read John 6:44).

Christians recognize the voice of the Spirit when He convicts us regarding sin. Many of us have experienced the Spirit's work during a worship service; we were strongly convinced that Jesus was Lord and worthy to be praised. Some of us have felt the convicting work of the Spirit so powerfully that we wept in our desire to be made right with God. Others have felt called to missions. Still others have been convicted by the Spirit to forgive someone who has wronged them.

 Are you presently experiencing conviction? ❑ Yes ❑ No Do you realize this is God speaking to you? ❑ Yes ❑ No What is He saying?

_____

GUIDE

"Your ears shall hear a word behind you, saying, 'This is the way, walk in it.' Whenever you turn to the right hand or whenever you turn to the left" (Isa. 30:21).

" 'It shall come to pass that before they call, I will answer; and while they are still speaking, I will hear' " (Isa. 65:24).

When bewildered and searching for direction for myself, my family, or my church, many times I have opened my Bible and prayed, "Oh Spirit of God, guide me so I will know the truth of this situation!" Immediately Scriptures came to mind giving me a clear answer. I bowed in thanksgiving to God who had done such a wonderful work in me. Of course, my immediate _obedience_ to the Holy Spirit was crucial to experiencing God.

Christians are often taught that God does not give specific direction for people's daily lives. The problem with this teaching is that it is not biblical. God never came to anyone in Scripture to ask them what they would like to do for Him. God always confronted people with His agenda for their lives. Those who adjusted their lives to God's will experienced God working in and through them in a dimension they never could have anticipated.

A clear word of guidance in my life has come from two passages in Isaiah 30:21 and 65:24. Read these verses. They have assured me that the Spirit will guide me in every major decision in my life.

What do you sense the Spirit guiding you to do right now? Are there areas in your life for which you have not asked God's guidance? Do so now.

GLORIFY CHRIST

Scripture affirms that when we obey God's commands, He is glorified. Jesus said when we obeyed Him, God would be glorified (read Matt. 5:16). Jesus also said that if we would pray, He would answer and the Father would be glorified (read John 14:13). Read John 17:10. Jesus affirmed that the Father would reveal Himself in and through His disciples and as people saw Christ in them, the Heavenly Father would receive glory. One of the roles of the Spirit is to bring glory to Christ through His activity in your life. There is nothing more inherent to your nature or more deeply satisfying than bringing glory to God.

"Let your light so shine before men, that they may see your good works and glorify your Father in heaven" (Matt. 5:16).

" 'And whatever you ask in My name, that I will do, that the Father may be glorified in the Son' " (John 14:13).

" 'And all Mine are Yours, and Yours are Mine, and I am glorified in them' " (John 17:10).

 As a review, match the following names of the Spirit listed in the margin with their definitions below.

___ 1. Guide
___ 2. Helper
___ 3. Glorify Christ
___ 4. Spirit of Truth
___ 5. Teacher
___ 6. Reminder
___ 7. Spirit of Conviction

a. works in your life to exalt Christ to the world around you
b. reveals spiritual truth to you
c. confronts the sin in your life and convinces you that Jesus is Lord
d. brings to mind things God said to you in His word
e. reveals God's perspective of your situation to you
f. helps you to do things impossible on your own
g. leads your life into His activity around you

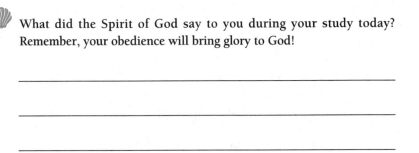 What did the Spirit of God say to you during your study today? Remember, your obedience will bring glory to God!

_____

_____

_____

What will you do as a result?

_____

_____

Answers: 1., g.; 2., f.; 3., a.; 4., e.; 5., b.; 6., d.; 7., c.

Day 3

BE FILLED WITH THE HOLY SPIRIT

" 'And being assembled together with them, He commanded them not to depart from Jerusalem, but to wait for the Promise of the Father, 'which,' He said, 'you have heard from Me; for John truly baptized with water, but you shall be baptized with the Holy Spirit not many days from now. But you shall receive power when the Holy Spirit has come upon you; and you shall be witnesses to Me in Jerusalem, and in all Judea and Samaria, and to the ends of the earth' " (Acts 1:4-5,8).

"The Spirit of the LORD shall rest upon Him, The Spirit of wisdom and understanding, The Spirit of counsel and might, The Spirit of knowledge and of the fear of the Lord" (Isa. 11:2).

Since the Holy Spirit is God's provision to guide us in knowing and doing His will, it is important that we have a deep relationship with Him. In many ways it is like any other relationship, only far more significant in outcome. For instance, in marriage, the more intimate the relationship, the stronger the marriage. If you were to ask God, "What do you want *most* of me?" God would not mention any job or activity. He would say, "Love the LORD your God with all your heart, with all your soul, and with all your strength" (Deut. 6:4-5) (see also Matt. 22:37; Mark 12:30; Luke 10:27).

No wonder Paul urged the believers to "be filled with the Spirit" (Eph. 5:18). That is, be personally, intimately, deeply related in every way to the Spirit of God. He will be to you what Jesus was to the disciples. Jesus said every disciple would be "baptized" with the Holy Spirit. The word *baptized* means *immersed* or *completely submerged*. Jesus urged and even commanded His disciples to be related to the Holy Spirit (read Acts 1:4-5,8). The term *immersed* indicates an extensive, personal relationship with the Holy Spirit which allows the Holy Spirit to be all God intended for us. When God's people were filled with the Holy Spirit they always: (1) knew when God was speaking, (2) knew what God was saying, and (3) were enabled to obey all God said. In the New Testament the Holy Spirit is a promise of God to every believer (Acts 2:1-21; 1 Cor. 12:3,12-14; Eph. 1:13-14). God speaks to us through His Spirit and gives wisdom, understanding, counsel, power, knowledge and fear of the Lord (read Isa. 11:2).

How can you be filled with the Spirit?
   BELIEVE that what God says about the Spirit is true.
   ASK God to work in you in all the ways He promised and purposed.
   YIELD all of your life to God and His work.
   LIVE your life in obedience to God's working in you daily.

Check yes or no after the following statements. Answer the follow-up questions.

* I believe what God says to me in Scripture. ❑ Yes ❑ No   If yes, how are you demonstrating your belief?

_____

* I am obeying what God is saying to me concerning the place and work of the Holy Spirit in my life. ❑ Yes ❑ No   If yes, how are you doing this?

_____

* I see evidence of the Holy Spirit's working in my life. ❑ Yes ❑ No   If yes, what is the evidence?

_____

If you are not satisfied with your responses, what is the Spirit saying to you?

What did God say to you during your study today?

_____

_____

What will you do as a result?

_____

_____

Day 4

BE LED BY THE SPIRIT

Paul urged, "Walk in the Spirit, and you shall not fulfill the lust of the flesh" (Gal. 5:16). Like marriage, when you live daily in harmony with each other, the

"However, when He, Spirit of truth, has come, He will guide you into all truth; for He will not speak on His own authority, but whatever He hears He will speak; and He will tell you things to come. He will glorify Me, for He will take of what is Mine and declare it to you. All things that the Father has are Mine. Therefore I said that He will take of Mine and declare it to you" (John 16:13-15).

"The Spirit Himself bears witness with our spirit that we are children of God, and if children, then heirs—heirs of God and joint heirs with Christ" (Rom. 8:16-17).

"Walk in the Spirit, and you shall not fulfill the lust of the flesh" (Gal. 5:16).

fullness of each life is shared and experienced by the other. This is true in the entire family as well. When you walk in harmony, love, and complete sacrifice of yourself to your family, each person experiences all you are and have to offer day after day. Each life is enriched. The expressions, *in Christ* and *in the Spirit* mean *in complete union with*. Jesus spoke of being in the Father and the Father in Him (see John 17:20-26). Jesus expressed this in a wonderful way, indicating His walk with the Father was the pattern for our walk with Him (John 15:7-12).

So it is with the Holy Spirit. We are to walk in the Spirit. If we do, the fullness of the Spirit will be real and active in us. Jesus expressed the magnitude of this relationship in John 16:13-15. Read those verses.

As the Holy Spirit works in your life, He will do two things which enable you to receive all the Father wants to give to you.

1. The Spirit will make you aware of the enormous riches God has at your disposal (read Rom 8:16-17). God loves you and desires to share with you the resources of heaven. The Spirit's role is to make you fully aware of the enormous resources available to you from the Father. It is possible to live a Christian life in defeat, joylessness, and fear because you are not aware of all that is at your disposal as a fellow heir with Christ.

2. The Spirit qualifies you to receive what the Father wants to give you. Psalm 84:11 promises, "No good thing will He withhold from those who walk uprightly." This being so, the Spirit is determined to help you "walk uprightly" so that you can receive God's best for your life (read Gal. 5:16). The Spirit will guide and convict you, preparing you to receive all that your Father has to give.

How important is it to walk in the Spirit? If you are walking in the Spirit, then all that belongs to Jesus will also be available to you. How do you do this?

Believe → Come to Christ → Hear → Obey → Experience

 How do you experience God working in you daily?

_____

Are you obeying God when He speaks to you? ❏ Yes ❏ No ❏ Sometimes   Recount one example of your obedience to God. Write a brief description below.

_____

_____

ALLOW THE SPIRIT TO PRODUCE FRUIT!

When my family moved to Saskatoon, my children discovered a garden in our back yard. It was springtime, and my four boys were curious to see what would grow once the snow melted. In the corner of the garden was a strange looking plant with large leaves and a red stem. Unknown to Marilynn and me, my children began to wonder if the plant was poisonous. They decided to conduct "scientific experiments" to see whether it was dangerous. After extensive "research" (involving pulling off leaves, stepping on it, and hitting it with a stick), they concluded it *was* poisonous and should be destroyed! They then tore the poor plant to pieces! To their surprise, several weeks later they discovered that this plant had *not* died and was now lush and full. They then learned that it was *not* poisonous but was a delicious fruit called rhubarb. With our limited income, our family could not afford much dessert, but Marilynn became an expert rhubarb pie baker! If it had not been for the determination of that plant to produce fruit, my family would have had many meals without dessert!

When the Spirit of God enters the life of a new Christian, His assignment is to produce spiritual fruit in that life. The more fruit that is produced, the more like Christ that person becomes. Galatians 5:22-23 describes the kind of fruit the Spirit is seeking to produce in every believer. Read those verses. Just as the rhubarb plant was *determined* to produce fruit in our garden, the Spirit of God is absolutely committed to producing fruit in your life.

"But the fruit of the Spirit is love, joy, peace, long-suffering, kindness, goodness, faithfulness, gentleness, self-control" (Gal. 5:22-23).

 Write briefly what the Spirit is saying to you about the development of spiritual fruit in your life. What has the Holy Spirit said about your (respond to at least two) ...

love? _____

_____

joy? _____

_____

peace? _____

_____

longsuffering? _____

_____

kindness? _____

_____

goodness? _____

_____

faithfulness? _____

_____

gentleness? _____

_____

self-control? _____

_____

Write John 16:13 from memory in the margin above.

What did God say to you during your study today?

_____

_____

What will you do as a result?

_____

_____

Day 5

BE OBEDIENT TO THE SPIRIT

Because we are commanded to be immersed in the Holy Spirit and to follow Him as our Guide and Counselor, we are confronted every day with the decision to obey or to disobey Him. The Bible explains that rejecting the words of the Holy Spirit for your life has consequences. The following are ways you can be disobedient to what God tells you by His Spirit.

RESISTING THE HOLY SPIRIT

At times, the word that comes from the Holy Spirit will be difficult. The Spirit will act like a surgeon, delicately removing from your life that which is making you spiritually sick. The Spirit may challenge your pride or confront you with how you have been wrong in your dealings with others. At times He will give you a clear direction as to what you should do in order to avoid anything that might lead to your destruction (read Prov. 16:25). The Spirit will lead you to make necessary corrections in your life so that you do not miss the immeasurable blessings God wants to give you.

"There is a way that seems right to a man, But its end is the way of death" (Prov. 16:25).

There may come a time when you will be unwilling to obey God's word. I have seen the devastating results in the lives of people who resisted the Holy Spirit. At first, resisting may not be easy to do. The word comes to your life; you know what you should do, but you resist. Then a new word comes, and you resist again. After a while, your heart that was so tender to a word from God becomes hardened. It becomes easier and easier to resist until you are no longer sensitive to God's word.

 Is there any way in which you may presently be resisting what the Holy Spirit is saying to you? If so, what is He saying to you that you are resisting?

GRIEVING THE HOLY SPIRIT

In Ephesians 4:30 Paul exhorted, "Do not grieve the Holy Spirit of God." Paul said this in the middle of a number of commands he had given regarding the Christian life. It appears in this context that Paul was concerned about those believers who *knew* what God wanted them to do but were unwilling to obey. Resisting the Spirit focuses upon our disobedience; grieving the Holy Spirit focuses upon the result of our disobedience.

If you consider your sin to be nothing more than breaking a rule, you may justify yourself by saying, "no one's perfect." If you view your sin as the failure to live by certain principles, you may take comfort in knowing that you can strive harder in the future. But, realizing that sin is an absolute betrayal of the Person who loves you deeply and sacrificially throws a whole new light on your sin.

One of the most vivid examples for me is the life of Hosea. Gomer, Hosea's wife, turned her back on the one person who had truly loved her in order to pursue those who only sought to use her. She resumed her immoral lifestyle. In one of the greatest chapters about love and forgiveness found in literature, God told the betrayed and rejected prophet to go and purchase her back from the slave block, return her to his home, and love her. What an incredible assignment! Yet, God was making a profound statement. God was saying, "Hosea, now you know how I feel every time My people, whom I have loved, reject Me and pursue their own desires." I tremble at such a word! To know that every time I sin, God views it as a rejection of Him personally. That causes me to be heartbroken over my sin, for I realize that I have *not* just broken a rule, I have grieved the Holy Spirit.

 Read Luke 19:41-44 in the margin. Circle words or phrases that identify how the disobedience of God's people in Jesus' day affected His heart. Honestly search your heart. Is there any way you might be grieving the Holy Spirit? If so, how are you doing that?

DON'T QUENCH THE HOLY SPIRIT
First Thessalonians 5:19 admonishes, "Do not quench the Spirit." The word *quench* means, *to put an end to, stop, drown out, put out, cool suddenly.* Although the Holy Spirit is present in a believer's life, His freedom to work and speak can be limited by the condition of the believer's heart. The Spirit of God is a *Holy* Spirit. He works most freely in a holy life. When you allow sin to fill you, the Spirit's work is "quenched." When you find the Spirit's activity and words to you becoming increasingly rare, you need to examine the condition of your heart.

 As you search your heart, could there be a way in which you are quenching the Spirit of God in your life? If so, how are you doing that?

 What did God say to you during your study this week?

_____

_____

"Now as He drew near, He saw the city and wept over it, saying, 'If you had known, even you, especially in this your day, the things that make for your peace! But now they are hidden from your eyes. For the days will come upon you when your enemies will build an embankment around you, surround you and close you in on every side, and level you, and your children within you, to the ground; and they will not leave in you one stone upon another, because you did not know the time of your visitation' " (Luke 19:41-44).

What will you do as a result?

_____

_____

A QUESTION OFTEN ASKED

I am not hearing God speak to me. Could it be that I have blasphemed the Holy Spirit? At times people fear they are not experiencing God speaking to them because they have inadvertently blasphemed the Holy Spirit. Read Matthew 12:31-32. The Spirit of God had worked mightily to heal a man who was demon-possessed. This was an occasion for the Spirit of God to reveal to the people watching who Jesus was. However, instead of recognizing and accepting the word from God, the Pharisees declared that Jesus had healed by the power of Satan. This was not an insult to Jesus but to the Spirit of God. They were refusing to accept the testimony from God as valid. Jesus warned that to reject and scorn the person and work of the Spirit of God could never be forgiven. This is not something a Christian can do. To become a genuine Christian, you must first acknowledge the absolute lordship of God over your life. To reject a word openly, repeatedly, and defiantly from God indicates you have not submitted yourself to Christ's lordship. If you are truly a Christian, you will not have blasphemed the Holy Spirit. However, if you are not experiencing God as you think you should, check to see if you have not resisted, grieved, or quenched the Holy Spirit.

" 'Therefore I say to you, every sin and blasphemy will be forgiven men, but the blasphemy against the Spirit will not be forgiven men. Anyone who speaks a word against the Son of Man, it will be forgiven him; but whoever speaks against the Holy Spirit, it will not be forgiven him, either in this age or in the age to come' " (Matt. 12:31-32).

37

Week 3

GOD SPEAKS THROUGH THE BIBLE

MEMORY VERSE

"All Scripture is given by inspiration of God, and is profitable for doctrine, for reproof, for correction, for instruction in righteousness, that the man of God may be complete, thoroughly equipped for every good work" (2 Tim. 3:16-17).

THIS WEEK'S LESSONS

Day 1: God's Word Is Our Guide
Day 2: God's Word Guided Jesus
Day 3: God's Word Guided the Early Church
Day 4: God's Word Is Experienced
Day 5: God's Word Is Our Life

SUMMARY OF WEEK 3

This week you will:
- identify God's sequence in speaking through Scripture;
- discover the importance of a daily quiet time;
- examine the scriptural profile of the church; and,
- experience the impact of Scripture on life experiences.

GOD'S WORD SPEAKS AND WE OBEY

The Spirit of God speaks through Scripture to help us know the will of God. During a difficult time in my life, I was trying to figure out what I should do. I read Psalm 50:15: "Call upon Me in the day of trouble; I will deliver you, and you shall glorify Me." That passage caused me to reflect on other times in the Bible when God delivered His people. The Holy Spirit impressed on me that I had not called unto the Lord. So I called unto God through prayer and gave my problem to Him. I also shared with Marilynn what I had done and she affirmed my actions and became an encourager. God answered in a wonderful way, and He was honored as a result. I heard God and obeyed Him, and God did for me what He said He would do through that Scripture!

Likewise, a lady came to me after a church service and told me she was to see her lawyer the next week about proceeding toward divorce. The Holy Spirit led me to share a Scripture with her. We turned to Malachi 2:16: "For the LORD God of Israel says that He hates divorce." I knew the Holy Spirit could take the Scripture and help her know the will of God, if she would listen and obey. Her response was shock and grief. She said, "I did not know this! No one told me!" We read other Scriptures on reconciliation. She wept and asked me to pray with her. We prayed together for several minutes. After our prayer, she said, "Tomorrow I am telling my lawyer to stop divorce proceedings. I am going to ask God to help me reconcile with my husband." The Spirit had taken the Word of God and impressed upon this woman that this was God's word to her.

Day 1

GOD'S WORD IS OUR GUIDE

In seeking God's will, the Bible is your clearest and most unmistakable source. Psalm 119 is a classic description of the way God uses Scripture to guide your life. Read Psalm 119:9,11,112. David recognized that God's word was best. When God brought to his attention the fact that his life was not in conformity with Scripture, David adjusted his life to match the standard and instruction of God's Word.

God often will use Scripture to speak to you. This might be during your quiet time or a sermon. The Holy Spirit may remind you of a specific verse at your workplace, on a billboard, or in the lyrics of a song. The Holy Spirit makes you aware that this Scripture has significance for you. You will experience a holy restlessness as you realize you must adjust your life to what Scripture says.

God wants to say many things to you through His Word. God may confront your sin or reveal something about Himself to enable you to love and trust Him more. God could bring Scripture to mind to alert you to something He knows you will encounter. God's Word can bring comfort in times of crisis.

When God speaks to you through His Word, a sequence occurs.

1. God gives you His Word.
2. You read or hear the Word of God, the Bible.
3. The Spirit reveals truth about God and His activity in and around you.
4. You adjust your life to the truth concerning God.
5. You obey God.
6. God works in and through you to accomplish His purposes.

Each time you respond in obedience to what God reveals, He speaks to you further about His will.

AN ILLUSTRATION

As you are having your quiet time, you read Matthew 10:20,32-33. Later, you go to the hairstylist. During your conversation she begins to talk about spiritual things. You realize this is the perfect time to share the difference Christ has made in your life. However, you are nervous. What if she laughs or criticizes your belief? The Spirit reminds you what He taught you that morning. You thought the Spirit was just giving you a devotional thought. You were unaware until now He was preparing you to share the gospel with someone that day.

"How can a young man cleanse his way? By taking heed according to Your word. ... Your word I have hidden in my heart, That I might not sin against You. ... I have inclined my heart to perform Your statutes Forever, to the very end" (Ps. 119:9,11,112).

"It is not you who speak, but the Spirit of your Father who speaks in you. ... Therefore whoever confesses Me before men, him I will also confess before My Father who is in heaven. But whoever denies Me before men, him I will also deny before My Father who is in heaven" (Matt. 10:20,32-33).

🐚 Briefly describe an experience from your life when God worked in you to accomplish His purpose.

_____

_____

God knows His assignment for you each day. He knows what trials or crises you will face. God knows each person you will meet and the needs they have. To prepare you, God speaks a word of guidance, caution, warning, or encouragement (check this week's memory verse). Always connect what God tells you in His word with what happens the rest of the day. When you do, you will find that in moments of anxiety, God's Word will give you peace. When a friend shares a concern, you will have a Scripture to give. Allow God to alert you each day through His Word to all He will be doing through your life personally, in your family, at your job, and in your church or mission field.

🐚 What might God want to prepare you for if, during your time spent in the Bible, He draws your attention to the following verses? Match the verse with the appropriate situation in the margin.

___ 1. Critical of a co-worker.

___ 2. Angry words toward a family member.

___ 3. Excessive concern over a personal issue.

a. "He who guards his mouth preserves his life, But he who opens wide his lips shall have destruction" (Prov. 13:3).

b. "Be anxious for nothing, but in everything by prayer and supplication, with thanksgiving, let your requests be made known to God" (Phil. 4:6).

c. "Why do you look at the speck in your brother's eye, but do not consider the plank in your own eye?" (Matt. 7:3).

🐚 What did God say to you during your study today?

_____

What will you do as a result?

_____

Answers: 1. c.; 2. a.; 3. b.

Day 2

GOD'S WORD GUIDED JESUS

Jesus modeled for us the way each believer should live before God. From birth to death, Jesus allowed Scripture to shape and guide His ministry.

- Jesus' birth happened in such a way "that it might be fulfilled which was spoken by the Lord" (Matt. 1:22).
- Jesus' parents were guided by the Scriptures in presenting Him in the temple (see Luke 2:21-24), in escaping to Egypt (see Matt. 2:13-15), and returning to Nazareth (see Matt. 2:23).
- John the Baptist prepared the way for Jesus in fulfillment of Scriptures (see Isa. 40:3-5; Luke 3:4-6).
- Jesus' responses to temptation were from Scripture (see Matt. 4:1-10).
- Jesus read from Scripture to announce the nature of His ministry, and then He followed it to the letter (see Luke 4:14-21).
- The Sermon on the Mount is filled with references to the Scriptures (see Matt. 5-7).
- Jesus responded to critics (see Matt. 9:13), identified God's work in others (see Matt. 11:10), and based His actions (see Matt. 12:1-8) on Scripture.
- The reason Jesus spoke in parables was to fulfill Scripture (see Matt. 13:14-15,34-35).
- Jesus cleansed the temple to bring it in line with what Scripture said (see Matt. 21:13).
- The details of Jesus' death fulfilled Scripture (Matthew 26:24,31,54,56; 27:9,34-35,46; John 19:36-37).

 What Scriptures are being used by God in your life right now?

Write this week's Scripture memory verse (2 Timothy 3:16-17) in the space below.

MY TIME WITH GOD

As I seek to pattern my life according to Scripture, I have some practices which help me immerse myself in God's Word. Let me share what I do.

1. Rise early, with plenty of time to be unhurried before God. God deserves unhurried and concentrated time. (Of course, the time you meet God will depend on your schedule.)
2. Meet God at a regular place and time each day.

3. Begin with a short prayer acknowledging my love relationship with God, and my dependence on Him. I review God's promises often.

4. Stand before God in His Word for:
   - instructions, standards, or guidelines for my life (Amos 7:7).
   - a fresh word from God.
   - a cleansing, as His Word addresses my sin (see Eph. 5:25-26).
   - God's provision for me in Christ (Col. 1:27-29; 2:2-3,6-7,9-10). Since God's provision for me is Christ, I read portions each day of one of the Gospels until completed to know Jesus more thoroughly.
   - exposure to the entire counsel of Scripture. I read from the Psalms, Proverbs, or passages from the Law, Prophets, and letters of the New Testament.

The amount of time I spend in God's Word depends on what God is impressing on me. There are times when I cannot leave until God releases me.

5. Use a notepad to record what the Spirit is teaching me. I do the following:
   - Write down what God says to me, including any adjustments I must make in order to be obedient. I review previous notes to see how God has been faithful to His word to me.
   - Stop and pray about what the Spirit has revealed of His will and respond by writing down my specific prayer response.
   - If I sense the magnitude of the Word from God, I go no further in the Scripture, but immediately meditate, writing down my thoughts as I align each area of my life with the truths revealed.
   - Place the truth alongside my life, mind, will, heart, call, and growth in Christ to see what adjustments I have to make to bring every area of my life into alignment with God's Word.
   - Place the truth beside my relationships with my spouse, children, co-workers, and ministry assignments.
   - Record any response I must make to incorporate what God has shown me. Review these notes regularly to hold myself accountable to the commitments I made to God.

6. After unhurried time in God's Word, spend time in prayer. My praying is based on God's Word. I pray about what the Spirit revealed. I also go to my regular prayer commitments. I end with thanksgiving and commitment, ready to obey.

Each person must develop his or her own approach to God's Word. This has been my basic approach for years and has led to many life-changing experiences with God and His Word. You may find another time of the day is better for you than the morning. You may not have the time to do all that I do every day. What is important is that you have a regular, adequate time with God.

What has been your process? Briefly describe your process by outlining it in the margin.

If you are not enjoying a rich time of fellowship with God in His Word, what adjustments do you intend to make? Review my list and circle the number by those that you will commit to implement.

Write a prayer response to God, committing yourself to spend regular and adequate time in His Word each day.

_____

_____

GOD'S WORD GUIDED THE EARLY CHURCH

Once Jesus returned to the Father, His disciples no longer had His physical presence to build His church. Yet, Jesus said *He* would build His church (read Matt. 16:18). In Acts we find a new pattern in the way God led His people. The Spirit of God took the Word of God and revealed to the church what it should do. Scripture was the early church's only textbook. The Holy Spirit led them to the Scriptures for practical guidance for whatever they were facing as a church.

Throughout Acts, the church was led by the Spirit through Scripture.

Acts 1—The church grappled with their hostile environment and the betrayal of Judas. Using Scripture, Peter guided the church to understand the events of their day and how to replace Judas.

Acts 2—Peter declared to the people of Jerusalem how Scripture had been fulfilled in the life of Jesus. This impacted his listeners so profoundly that 3,000 people were added to the church!

Acts 3—Peter and John healed a lame man. When a crowd gathered, they explained the miraculous events of the day based on Scripture.

Acts 4—The religious professionals of the day challenged the actions of Peter, and Peter responded from Scripture. So convinced was Stephen of what God had said to him that he fearlessly faced death in Acts 7.

Acts 8—Philip was led by the Spirit to share his faith with the Ethiopian eunuch. He shared Scripture with him which led to the eunuch's conversion.

The church today is just as dependent upon the Spirit of God to guide it by Scripture, so that it will know how to be all that God wants it to be.

" 'And I also say to you that you are Peter, and on this rock I will build My church, and the gates of Hades shall not prevail against it' " (Matt. 16:18).

FOR FURTHER STUDY
Read the following passages and write other words in the margin below that describe what the church should be like.
- Matthew 16:18
- 1 Corinthians 12:25-26
- Ephesians 4:32
- Colossians 3:16
- 1 Timothy 4:13
- James 5:16

YOU AND YOUR CHURCH AND GOD'S WORD

The following exercises will help you gain a clear picture of the place of Scripture in your life and church. This may be an exercise that challenges your thinking. Allow the Holy Spirit to teach you through His Word.

 Read the following verses, and underline words that describe what the church ought to be like. These two passages begin to describe God's church (for other descriptors, see For Further Study).

" 'Go therefore and make disciples of all the nations, baptizing them in the name of the Father and of the Son and of the Holy Spirit, teaching them to observe all things that I have commanded you; and lo, I am with you always, even to the end of the age' " (Matt. 28:19-20).

"Then those who gladly received his word were baptized; and that day about three thousand souls were added to them. And they continued steadfastly in the apostles' doctrine and fellowship, in the breaking of bread, and in prayers. Then fear came upon every soul, and many wonders and signs were done through the apostles. Now all who believed were together, and had all things in common, and sold their possessions and goods, and divided them among all, as anyone had need. So continuing daily with one accord in the temple, and breaking bread from house to house, they ate their food with gladness and simplicity of heart, praising God and having favor with all the people. And the Lord added to the church daily those who were being saved" (Acts 2:41-47).

What underlined characteristics describe your church? Circle them.

How diligently are you letting Scripture guide and shape both your church's message and methods? ❏ none ❏ somewhat ❏ entirely

Are you guiding the children in your church to know how Scriptures help them know when God is speaking and how to recognize His ways?
❏ Yes How?

❏ No   What can you do to begin giving guidance to your children in this area?

_____

Is the study of Scripture in your church ❏ a tradition or ❏ a careful guide to experiencing God and His ways and will for your lives daily? Explain your answer.

_____

_____

Do you take your Bible to church? ❏ Yes ❏ No If you do, how do you use it once you arrive?

_____

Do the children and youth in your church guide their lives by Scripture? ❏ Yes ❏ No What evidence do you see in their lives to support your answer?

_____

How do you perceive the adults in your church guiding their lives in the workplace by Scripture?

_____

_____

What did God say to you during your study today?

_____

_____

What will you do as a result?

_____

Day 4

GOD'S WORD IS EXPERIENCED

" 'Eye has not seen, nor ear heard, Nor have entered into the heart of man The things which God has prepared for those who love Him.' But God has revealed them to us through His Spirit. For the Spirit searches all things, yes, the deep things of God. For what man knows the things of man except the spirit of the man which is in him? Even so no one knows the things of God except the Spirit of God. Now we have received, not the spirit of the world, but the Spirit who is from God" (1 Cor. 2:9-12).

God's Word was not just for the Israelites, Jesus, and the early church. The Word of God is alive even now. It is not given that we might know about God, but that we might experience Him. To know God with the head is dry and impersonal. To have an emotional experience apart from Scripture is shallow and potentially heretical. To encounter God in His Word, however, gives us the clear and unerring guidance we need for our lives. The Spirit knows the mind of God and what the Father has in store for you (1 Cor. 2:9-12).

Do the following when God leads you to a fresh understanding of Himself, His purposes, or His ways through Scripture.

1. Write down the verse(s) in a spiritual journal or diary. Assume that whenever God says something to you, the message is worth recording.
2. Meditate on the verse. Some truths of God are so profound, they cannot be understood with a light reading of the Bible. You need the truth of God to have time to penetrate your life and heart.
3. Study the meaning of the verse(s). What is God revealing about Himself, His purposes, or His ways?
4. Identify the adjustments you need to make in your personal life, your family, your church, and your work so God can work in you.
5. Write a prayer response to God.
6. Make the necessary adjustments to God, and obey what He has said.
7. Watch to see how God uses that truth about Himself in your life.

 Practice this process with this week's memory verse. First, write it in the margin.

What does this passage reveal to you about God, His purposes, and His ways?

_____

_____

Meditate on this passage and pray. Ask God to continue speaking to you about the truth in this passage. Keep in mind that God is more interested in what you become than in what you do.

What adjustments would you have to make to align your life with His truth in your …

personal life? _____

family life? _____

church life?_____

work life? _____

Write a prayer response in the margin to God expressing your willingness to obey and apply this truth.

Since you first came to understand this truth, has God done anything in your life that required you to apply the truth or share it with someone else? ❑ Yes ❑ No If God has seemingly done nothing yet, pray that you will be sensitive to how God wants to apply this truth.

Day 5

GOD'S WORD IS OUR LIFE

 Read the following verses and underline in each one the significance God's Word has for your life.

"Set your hearts on all the words which I testify among you today, which you shall command your children to be careful to observe—all the words of this law. For it is not a futile thing for you, because it is your life" (Deut. 32:46-47).

"This Book of the Law shall not depart from your mouth, but you shall meditate on it day and night, that you may observe to do according to all that is written in it. For then you will make your way prosperous, and then you will have good success" (Josh. 1:8).

"It is the Spirit who gives life; the flesh profits nothing. The words that I speak to you are spirit, and they are life" (John 6:63).

"If you abide in Me, and My words abide in you, you will ask what you desire, and it shall be done for you" (John 15:7).

How does God's word bring life? At times, it can literally bring life, as when Jesus said "Lazarus, come forth!" and death was immediately subjected to the authority of God. As our daughter turned 16, we were informed that she had cancer. These were words of "death." However, as we immersed ourselves in God's Word, Marilynn and I sensed that the Spirit was telling us the same thing Jesus once assured His disciples: "This sickness is not unto death" (John 11:4). We received letters from others who sensed God leading them to this same verse for our daughter. We knew this was not always God's word for those with cancer, but in our situation, God's Spirit assured us that this was His word. Our daughter was healed, and we realized God's words had brought life.

God's Word can bring "life" by bringing hope. When God's people were in captivity and their situation appeared hopeless, God's Word brought "life" by giving them hope. Read Isaiah. 41:10.

"Fear not, for I am with you; Be not dismayed, for I am your God. I will strengthen you, Yes, I will help you, I will uphold you with My righteous right hand" (Isa. 41:10).

I still remember the times, as a young man, when I was told my parents had died. God sent His Word to comfort me so that at these difficult times in my life, I experienced victory and hope. Only a word from God can do that.

God's Word can bring us "life" by protecting us from death. God's Word came to the sons-in-law of Lot to escape Sodom. Their lives depended on their immediate obedience (see Gen. 19:14). God's word came to Lot's wife that she was not to look back on the city as she fled (see Gen. 19:17,26). If these people had obeyed God's word, they would have experienced life. Instead, they faced immediate death. The Bible has been misunderstood as a book of rules designed to prevent people from having fun. It is just the opposite. The Bible protects people from death.

PROMISES OF GOD'S WORD

If you found yourself in a war-torn country and had to pass through a minefield to return to safety, your life would be in enormous peril. One wrong step would have disastrous consequences! If a soldier approached you while you stood in the middle of the minefield and handed you a map marking the location of the mines, those instructions would immediately become the most important information in your life. The rules you had to follow would not discourage you. So God's Word, when followed and implemented, brings you out of death into full and abundant life.

God's Word is brimming with promises which are available to bring you life. Think of some of the promises God has made to you and the incredible life He gives when you believe Him.

Read the following verses in your Bible and match each verse with the promise God's word offers you.

___ 1. Jeremiah 33:3   a. The Lord brings comfort in all situations.
___ 2. Psalm 23   b. God will supply all our needs through
___ 3. Romans 8:37   Christ.
___ 4. 2 Corinthians 9:8   c. God's grace provides for all good work.
___ 5. Philippians 4:19   d. Call on the Lord and the Lord will hear.
___ 6. John 14:12-14   e. God will do anything we ask in His name.
                           f. God's love conquers all.

The full expression of the love of God flows into and through your life when you know His commands and practice them faithfully. God's words are your life! Just as surely as God spoke and life came to persons in His day, so He brings life to you when you read the Scriptures, learn what He commands, and do it.

What Scriptures has God given you that have given you life?

_____

_____

How has God used Scriptures to guide you?

_____

_____

What did God say during your study this week?

_____

_____

What will you do as a result?

_____

_____

FOR FURTHER STUDY
David was aware that Scriptures were his life. That is, God would bless with abundant life only when he followed and obeyed God's Word. Read the following verses from Psalm 119. List what David said about the Word of God and his commitment to God's word.

vv. 2-3 _____
vv. 9-11 _____
vv. 18,27 _____
vv. 30-32 _____
vv. 33-37 _____
vv. 44-45 _____
vv. 54-56 _____
v. 59 _____
vv. 67,71 _____
vv. 105,120 _____
v. 148 _____

Answers: 1. d.; 2. a.; 3. f.; 4. c.; 5. b.; 6. e.

A QUESTION OFTEN ASKED

I want to order my life according to Scripture, but how do I know if I am picking a certain verse in the Bible just so I can justify doing what I want? First, never use just one Scripture to justify your action! If God is revealing a truth about Himself, you will be overwhelmed with many Scriptures saying the same thing.

Second, spend time in prayer. God will affirm His Word to you there.

Third, share with others what you believe God is saying. You may indeed have a "blind spot" (i.e., your will, rather than His). Others may have a clear affirmation, or warning, or caution. Take their word seriously.

Fourth, if you have any doubts, don't proceed until God gives you peace of mind.

Week 4

GOD SPEAKS THROUGH PRAYER

MEMORY VERSE

"Call to Me, and I will answer you, and show you great and mighty things, which you do not know" (Jer. 33:3).

THIS WEEK'S LESSONS

Day 1: Prayer Is a Relationship
Day 2: Prayer Changes Us
Day 3: Prayer Is Answered in Different Ways
Day 4: Prayer May Be Hindered
Day 5: Prayer Requires Spiritual Concentration

SUMMARY OF WEEK 4

This week you will:

• learn God's pattern in prayer;
• evaluate your relationship with God in light of your prayer life;
• distinguish God's three answers to prayer; and,
• identify any hindrances to your prayer life.

GOD ANSWERED WHILE RICHARD PRAYED

When Richard was in college, he sensed the need to consecrate his life to God. One day as he was spending a wonderful time with the Lord in prayer, sincerely committing himself to do whatever God told him, the phone rang. It was a troubled, lonely young man who often called church people to talk. Richard was annoyed! This person always seemed to call at the wrong time. Richard had been thoroughly presenting himself for God's service and was disappointed at the interruption! Only later did he connect his prayer with the phone call. God answered Richard's prayer even before he said "amen."

We need to pray with a sense of expectancy, knowing that God answers prayer and that if we ask Him to direct our paths, He will. Often we pray for an opportunity to serve God, but when this opportunity comes, we see it as an interruption rather than God's answer. Sometimes the opportunity God brings will not have all the excitement we desire, but if we pray and ask God to speak to us, we must be willing to respond to what He does next.

Day 1

PRAYER IS A RELATIONSHIP

"I sought the LORD, and He heard me, And delivered me from all my fears. They looked to Him and were radiant, And their faces were not ashamed. This poor man cried out, and the Lord heard him, And saved him out of all his troubles. The angel of the LORD encamps all around those who fear Him, And delivers them. Oh, taste and see that the LORD is good; Blessed is the man who trusts in Him" (Ps. 34:4-8).

Prayer is a relationship, not an activity. When Jesus taught His disciples to pray, He did not choose the words "Lord," or "Almighty God" to begin His prayer, even though these would have been appropriate terms to address God. Instead, Jesus prayed: "Our Father …" What could be more personal or loving than a relationship with God as our Heavenly Father?

The first two words of Jesus' model prayer imply a relationship (see Matt. 6:9-13). First, *our,* gives us an awareness of the significance of praying with others and identifying with others. Jesus was teaching always to have your brother in mind when you pray.

Second, *Father* demonstrates an intimate, trusting, and loving relationship with God. It indicates you do not merely say prayers, do your duty, or exercise a discipline, but you converse with a Person. This name anticipates conversation—listening and hearing from God!

Have you ever had a conversation with someone who did all the talking? It can be frustrating wanting to tell your concerns, but never having the opportunity. Do you approach God expecting conversation? Do you wait for Him to speak when you have finished talking?

Every prayer recorded in the Bible is personal, specific, and powerful. Prayer is the same today. We must never let it deteriorate to empty religion as the Israelites did (Isa. 1:10-17; Matt. 15:8-9), or to "vain repetition" (Matt. 6:7).

The purpose of prayer is not to influence God, but to change us. A classic example was Moses on Mount Sinai. Moses was called into God's presence through prayer. God revealed that the people had sinned so grievously that He was going to destroy them. This word changed Moses, and he began to intercede with God. God heard Moses and spared the people.

"So I sought for a man among them who would make a wall, and stand in the gap before Me on behalf of the land, that I should not destroy it; but I found no one. Therefore I have poured out My indignation on them; I have consumed them with the fire of My wrath" (Ezek. 22:30-31).

When God knows He must judge a people, He looks for a person who is intimate with Him in prayer. Why? So He can show mercy to others as the person prays and intercedes. How tragic when God looks in vain for someone to intercede with Him (read Ezek. 22:30-31).

How is your time of prayer personal and real?

_____

_____

How do you sense God's presence and voice as you pray?

_____

_____

How do you listen when you pray?

_____

_____

What did God say to you during your study today?

_____

_____

What will you do as a result?

_____

_____

Day 2

PRAYER CHANGES US

As a pastor, I habitually began my week by praying for my congregation. During this prayer time, God would bring specific individuals to my mind. Though I did not always know their circumstances, I would sense the Holy Spirit leading me to pray especially for them. After my prayer time, I would write notes to those for whom I had prayed. Invariably, I would receive word later in the week from these people telling me that they had been in the midst of difficulties. My note came at just the right time, giving them the assurance and promise from God they needed. Often there was no way I could have known that they would lose their job that week, that their child would become ill, or that pressures in the home would mount, but the Spirit of God knew and alerted me as I prayed.

Scripture shows that God generally follows a pattern when He speaks to us through prayer.

1. God takes the initiative by causing us to want to pray.
2. The Holy Spirit reveals the will of God through the Word of God.
3. We pray in agreement with the will of God.
4. We adjust our lives to the truth of God.
5. We look and listen for confirmation or further direction from the Bible, circumstances, and the church (other believers).
6. We obey.
7. God works in and through us to accomplish His purposes.
8. We experience God just as the Holy Spirit revealed.

Many people could testify that while they were praying, God brought to mind a certain person. Sometimes they were told to phone or visit someone. Sometimes they recalled a specific Scripture they were to share. As they obeyed, God brought salvation to some, encouragement to others, or specific words of direction. God has always done this. Are you expecting God to speak and give clear guidance to you as you pray?

Write Jeremiah 33:3, the memory verse for this week, three times in the margin.

 Write a brief example of God's speaking and giving clear guidance to you. What happened when you obeyed?

_____

_____

Day 3

PRAYER IS ANSWERED IN DIFFERENT WAYS

God communicates with us powerfully in response to our prayers. Have you ever prayed and asked God to do something and then been surprised when He did it? Do you remember when the church in Jerusalem prayed for Peter while he was in prison? While the church prayed, Peter arrived at their door, having been released miraculously. When the people were told that Peter was standing at the door, their response was, "You are beside yourself!" (Acts 12:15). Poor Peter had to continue knocking while the church debated whether God had answered their prayers! When the people finally saw Peter, "they were astonished" (Acts 12:16).

What about Zacharias? He and his wife Elizabeth had never had children. On his appointed day to enter the temple to burn incense, he was met by the angel Gabriel. Gabriel said, "Do not be afraid, Zacharias, for your prayer is heard" (Luke 1:13). His prayers had been heard. Yet, do you remember his response? Zacharias had so much disbelief that the angel made him mute until the day his son was delivered. Should we ever be surprised when God responds to our prayers? Surprise on our part may indicate a lack of belief.

We find many verses in the Bible on prayer. The following verses are representative of the many that indicate what God promises He will do when we pray.

" 'Call to Me, and I will answer you, and show you great and mighty things, which you do not know' " (Jer. 33:3).

"Whatever things you ask in prayer, believing, you will receive" (Matt. 21:22).

"Ask, and it will be given to you; seek, and you will find; knock, and it will be opened to you" (Luke 11:9-13).

"If you abide in Me, and My words abide in you, you will ask what you desire, and it shall be done for you" (John 15:7).

"Most assuredly, I say to you, whatever you ask the Father in My name He will give you" (John 16:23).

"Whatever we ask we receive from Him, because we keep His commandments and do those things that are pleasing in His sight" (1 John 3:22).

 Go back and underline what our responsibilities are if we hope to receive God's answer to our prayers.

Now, circle the words or phrases that indicate what God says He will do when we pray.

The Bible is explicit about what happens when we pray. God teaches us things we did not know. God grants us what we asked Him for. He answers our prayer. Be careful you do not fail to recognize God in the midst of His answer to you. Sometimes you can be so delighted with what you receive that you fail to recognize that God has communicated with you.

GOD REVEALED HIS LOVE IN HIS ANSWER TO PRAYER

Richard and Lisa came to a time of great need when they were attending seminary. They only had one day's supply of baby food for their son and would not be able to purchase more for another week. As they prayed, God gave them a sense of peace that He had heard their prayer. Moments later the telephone rang. It was a young woman who worked with Lisa. The woman was embarrassed and apologized profusely. She said, "I hope you are not offended. I have never done this before. But, my baby has suddenly refused to eat baby food. I have shelves and shelves of baby food that I would be happy to bring to work for you tomorrow if you could use it." The next evening Lisa returned home with dozens of jars of baby food! Richard and Lisa spontaneously rejoiced as they realized God had answered their prayers in a practical way. In the process, God reminded them of His love for them.

Describe a time you know that God answered your prayer.

_____

_____

How were you aware that the answer was God communicating His love to you?

_____

_____

It may seem simplistic, but when God answers your request, it is always *yes, yes, but not yet,* or *no.*

YES

The question is not whether God responds, but what does He say? At times, God's answer to you may be yes. What an incredible experience it is when your Heavenly Father says yes to your request! God loves us and willingly gives us those things which are best for our lives.

Recount a time when God said yes to a prayer you prayed. Write a brief description about it in the margin.

YES, BUT NOT YET

There may be times when, in God's wisdom, He acknowledges the worthiness of your request, but determines that the timing is not right. There have been times when sincere people prayed and received an assurance that God would grant their request, but then nothing seemed to happen. When God speaks to us, we have an obligation to stay with that word until it comes to pass.

Abram waited 25 years for the child promised by God. David waited many years after he was anointed king before he ever sat on the throne. Paul had a miraculous encounter with Christ and yet spent several years in the desert before being sent out as a missionary. Some of the people who experienced the greatest ministries are those who had to wait upon God to bring it to pass.

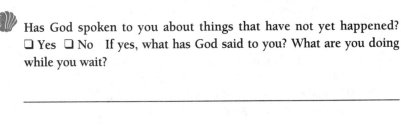 **Has God spoken to you about things that have not yet happened? ❏ Yes ❏ No   If yes, what has God said to you? What are you doing while you wait?**

_____

_____

NO

We need to be reminded that no *is* an answer! At times we can become frustrated because God has not "answered" our prayer. If we are sensitive to what God is saying, we will realize God has spoken to us; His answer is "no!" God loves us too much to grant some of our requests.

Marilynn and I raised five children. At times one of them would try to convince us that it would be best if he did not go to school one day or that he should eat ice cream for breakfast. He might accuse us of not loving him because we did not give him what he asked for. We always answered; sometimes we chose to say no. It was futile for our children to say to themselves, "Well, my father has not given me what I asked for, but if I persist in asking, and I ask believing, then eventually I *will* receive what I am asking for!" We did not give in if they did this. Rather, we felt disappointed that they did not know and trust us well enough to believe we were doing what was best for them.

We read in Acts 12 how the church prayed and how Peter was delivered miraculously. Notice that immediately before this account, James was imprisoned by the same King Herod. I imagine the church prayed for James' release as fervently as they did for Peter's. Yet, James was beheaded. For Peter, God's answer was yes. For James, it was no.

Some teach that if we simply persist in our prayers, God will grant our requests. Some refuse to take no as an answer. However, it is an affront to God to keep praying for something when God has said no. The purpose of prayer is not to conform God to our will, but to conform us to His. If God says no, we must trust that God's perfect love always provides us with the perfect answer. If you ever wonder how a loving God could say no to His children's request, you only have to revisit Jesus in the garden of Gethsemane. There, facing the horror of a brutal death, Jesus prayed, "O My Father, if it is possible, let this cup pass from Me" (Matt. 26:39). Even though God loved His Son deeply, He knew from His eternal perspective that He must allow Jesus to go to the cross to redeem the lost. God applies His eternal, redemptive perspective to each of our requests. When His answer is no, there is far more at stake than we realize.

Have you ever earnestly prayed for something and then, later, been thankful God did not grant your request?

At times, I prayed in a certain direction, thinking I knew what would be best. As time unfolded, I saw more clearly what God was doing. I realized that my request would not have been appropriate for the mighty work God intended to do. I thank God for saying no and for giving me something far better. When God says no, it is because He has something far better for us (read Eph. 3:20).

"Now to Him who is able to do exceedingly abundantly above all that we ask or think, according to the power that works in us, to Him be glory in the church by Christ Jesus to all generations, forever and ever" (Eph. 3:20).

Have you been asking God for something that He has not granted? ❑ Yes ❑ No If yes, what is it?

_____

_____

Why might God be saying no to your request?

_____

_____

What did God say to you during your study today?

_____

_____

What will you do as a result?

_____

_____

PRAYER MAY BE HINDERED

At times God may be silent as you pray to Him. Scripture warns that there are hindrances to prayer. God may be refusing to hear your prayer because of the condition of your life.

Before you begin today's study, repeat Jeremiah 33:3 three times from memory and then write it in the margin below.

SIN
Unconfessed sin is perhaps the fastest way to short circuit your prayer life.

 Read the following verses and underline the reasons for prayers not being answered.

"When you spread out your hands, I will hide my eyes from you; Even though you make many prayers, I will not hear. Your hands are full of blood" (Isa. 1:15).

"If I regard iniquity in my heart, The Lord will not hear" (Ps. 66:18).

Scripture gives a graphic picture of how God sees our sin and how it affects our relationship with Him. Isaiah 1:15 presents a murderer who, with the blood of his victim still on his hands, goes to worship and asks God for a blessing! When a pious Jew prayed, he held his hands up in the air to signify to God that he had not committed any sin with his hands. The people in Isaiah 1 were oblivious to their sins. They did not notice that their hands which they were holding up to God dripped with their victim's blood. God said He would not even look at the person praying or give them His attention as long as they refused to repent.

Does this happen today? Yes. Couples committing adultery pray and ask God to bless their relationship! Employers mistreat their employees and ask God to bless their business! People act selfishly and yet ask God to bless them!

Take a moment to reflect on your life. Is there any sin that could be causing God to refuse to answer your prayers? ❏ Yes ❏ No Confess that sin now and ask God's forgiveness.

RELATIONSHIPS

"Therefore if you bring your gift to the altar, and there remember that your brother has something against you, leave your gift there before the altar, and go your way. First be reconciled to you brother, and then come and offer your gift" (Matt. 5:23-24).

"Husbands, likewise, dwell with them [wives] with understanding, giving honor to the wife, as to the weaker vessel, and as being heirs together of the grace of life, that your prayers may not be hindered" (1 Pet. 3:7).

Another area that can hinder your prayer is your relationships. Jesus said it is futile for you to attempt to worship or speak to the Lord while your brother has something against you (read Matt. 5:23-24). Jesus saw people who offended and mistreated others stand in the synagogue and say pious prayers. Jesus condemned this hypocrisy and essentially said, "you are wasting your breath. First, be reconciled with your brother, and then come to worship and pray to God." Jesus did not say, "send a card and hope he gets over it." Or, "try to be reconciled but, if the person refuses, go on about your business." No, Jesus commanded, "Be reconciled!" Could your prayers be unanswered because after one attempt at reconciliation you assumed the problem was now the other person's, and you began to try to relate to God as if everything was now all right?

The way you treat your spouse affects your prayers (read 1 Pet. 3:7). One of God's protections for Christian marriage is a "warning system" for husbands. If a husband mistreats his wife, God alerts him by changing their prayer relationship.

 From the following list of relationships in your life, check those that have the most potential to hinder your prayer life. Prayerfully note any changes God wants you to make in them.

❏ Spouse ❏ Employer ❏ Brother/Sister
❏ Children ❏ Employee ❏ Church member
❏ Parents ❏ Co-worker ❏ Friend

RITUAL

"And when you pray, you shall not be like the hypocrites. For they love to pray standing in the synagogues and on the corners of the streets, that they may be seen by men. … And when you pray, do not use vain repetitions as the heathen do. For they think that they will be heard for their many words" (Matt. 6:5-8).

Another hindrance to your prayer life is religion verses relationship. Jesus warned His disciples not to be like the heathen who thought God would be impressed with "vain repetitions" (read Matt. 6:5-8). The heathen thought that by "saying prayers," God would be pleased. There is a difference between "saying prayers" and praying!

How would you describe your prayers? Check all that apply.
❏ monologue ❏ a list of demands
❏ reciting a formula ❏ a hurried visit
❏ angry accusations ❏ "Let's make a deal"
❏ listening to every word ❏ an intimate, two-way conversation

60

DISOBEDIENCE

A final area which can dramatically affect your prayers is your obedience. Amos warned that our disobedience could lead to a "famine" of words coming to you from God (read Amos 8:11).

For those people who heard what God wanted them to do but did not obey, Amos cautioned that there may come a time when God ceases to give a new word of instruction. When God tells you to obey, it is pointless for you to disobey and then ask Him to do something for you. At times, God's silence in your prayers may indicate that He is displeased about an act of disobedience.

Many people who are not Christians or who are not walking with the Lord become bitter when they pray and God does not answer. People who ignore God, His church, and His word have the audacity to become indignant that God does not respond when they pray! The only prayer they can expect God to answer is a prayer of repentance.

 Is disobedience in your life preventing God from speaking to you? ❑ Yes ❑ No If yes, what is it? What do you intend to do about this?

_____

_____

"'Behold, the days are coming,' says the Lord GOD, 'That I will send a famine on the land, Not a famine of bread, Nor a thirst for water, But of hearing the words of the LORD'" (Amos 8:11).

Silence can be one of the best ways for God to speak to you. It can be a warning that there is something wrong with your relationship. Be sensitive to what God is saying when silence occurs, and make any necessary adjustments so your fellowship with God in prayer can be restored.

Day 5

PRAYER REQUIRES SPIRITUAL CONCENTRATION

A young woman approached me after a church service and expressed concern that, although she had been praying, "nothing seems to be happening in my life!" I told her I did not see things the same way. I reminded her that, over the last few months, her unsaved husband had begun to attend church, her child was thoroughly enjoying Sunday School, she had been growing in her relationship with God, and God had been using her to minister to her neighborhood. Surprised, she said, "That's right! I guess God *is* answering my prayers!" This sincere woman was so focused on praying that she was oblivious to the answers God was showering upon her.

Spiritual concentration is essential to effective prayer. The problem arises when we pray and never relate our prayers to anything that happens next. Once God speaks, He sets in motion the fulfillment of what He spoke.

 State in your own words the promise God gives in the verses below. Write your response in the margin by the verse.

"The LORD of hosts has sworn, saying, 'Surely, as I have thought, so it shall come to pass, And as I have purposed, so it shall stand. For the LORD of hosts has purposed, And who will annul it? His hand is stretched out, And who will turn it back?' " (Isa. 14:24,27).

"Surely the Lord God does nothing, Unless He reveals His secret to His servants the prophets" (Amos 3:7).

When God determines to do something, He tells His people (read Amos 3:7). When God wants to do something in your family, at your workplace, with your neighbor, or in your child's school, He will alert you so that you can become involved in His work. Your spiritual concentration will help you connect what is happening to what God said to you earlier.

The story of Peter and Cornelius is instructive in showing how God guides us through prayer. Cornelius "prayed to God always" (Acts 10:2). One day as Cornelius prayed, God spoke to him and told him that his prayers had not gone unheard. God told Cornelius to send for Peter. At that same time Peter was praying in Joppa. While Peter prayed, God spoke to him and convicted him of his prejudice. Immediately after God spoke to Peter, there was a knock at the door. It was a Gentile. Peter did not fail to make the connection between what God had just said to him in prayer and what happened next!

Your spiritual concentration is essential if you are to recognize all that God is doing around you. I sensed the need to visit someone in the hospital who was not a Christian but postponed doing so until the next day. The person died suddenly during the night. Spiritual concentration when God speaks is critical. When you pray for God to give you an opportunity to share your faith, are you sensitive to the conversation you have with another parent at your child's sporting event, or to the neighbor who "just stopped by," or to a phone call you received that morning? As you pray for God's financial provision, do you make the connection with the opportunity for overtime posted at work that day, or the advice you received from someone at work that will save you some money, or the neighbors who bring you vegetables from their garden? Could you pray for God's presence in your life and then never recognize Him when, after receiving some difficult news, you experienced an unusual sense of peace filling your life? Could you pray for opportunities to minister to someone and then pass by person after person without ever recognizing they were filled with needs that you could meet?

If you are not careful, you can leave your place of prayer and never make the connection between your prayer and the events of your day.

 In the space below, list things you have been praying about in the column on the left. List events or circumstances which have occurred recently on the right. Draw a line connecting circumstances with things about which you have been praying.

Prayers	**Events/Circumstances**
• _____	• _____
• _____	• _____
• _____	• _____
• _____	• _____
• _____	• _____

If you have a prayer journal, review it and thank God for answered prayer. If you do not presently keep a prayer journal, begin doing so!

 What did God say to you as a result of your study this week?

_____

_____

What will you do as a result?

_____

_____

A QUESTION OFTEN ASKED

The Bible says that if I ask anything in Jesus' name, believing, that my prayer will be answered. I prayed for my mother who was extremely ill. My heart was "right" with God, but she died. Was it my fault that God did not heal my mother? First, to "ask in Jesus' name" means to ask in harmony with all you know of Him and in harmony with His nature and His ways.

Second, if you trusted God sincerely, accept His answer as an expression of His best, in love for you, and rejoice in His greater knowledge and His perfect love.

Third, often it takes time, looking back, to get the fuller picture of God's directives. It may not be until you are in heaven that you fully understand situations like these.

Fourth, in Scripture, whenever God's answer was no, He always had a bigger, eternal purpose (see Mark 14:35-36; Heb. 5:7-10).

GOD SPEAKS THROUGH CIRCUMSTANCES

MEMORY VERSE

"And we know that all things work together for good to those who love God, to those who are the called according to His purpose" (Rom. 8:28).

THIS WEEK'S LESSONS

Day 1: Circumstances: God at Work
Day 2: Circumstances: Spiritual Markers
Day 3: Circumstances: Confusing Apart from God
Day 4: Circumstances: Explained by God
Day 5: Circumstances: Open or Closed Doors

SUMMARY OF WEEK 5

This week you will:
• recognize God's work through circumstances;
• apply God's guidelines to confusing circumstances; and,
• distinguish between open and closed doors.

A CIRCUMSTANCE DEMANDING ATTENTION

I was teaching at a conference center one summer. A couple asked to speak with me. They recounted how God had blessed their business and family. They said, "Some years ago God seemed to be calling us into missions, but we had two life goals to accomplish first. We wanted to build and pay off our home, and we wanted to get our two children through the university." They told how they had paid off their home and were anticipating their children graduating. With tears in their eyes they said: "This year a tornado swept through our town. The only house destroyed was ours. Do you think God is speaking to us? What do you think we should do?" I replied, "Obey God immediately!" I encouraged them to pray through the rest of the afternoon and to be prepared to hear God speak to them as the president of our Foreign Mission Board preached that evening.

During the service, I sat near the front of the auditorium. During the altar call, the couple came weeping, but joyful. As they made their way with a counselor, I stepped out to greet them. They fell on my neck, saying, "There you are! We just said 'Yes. Lord' to God's call to missions!"

Circumstances! They can speak loudly and clearly to us about God's will if we will hear and obey Him.

Day 1

CIRCUMSTANCES: GOD AT WORK

Circumstances are events that occur in your life which God uses to speak clearly about Himself, His purposes, and His ways. When God speaks through your circumstances, it can dramatically affect what you are doing, thinking, or feeling. Circumstances can appear to be good, such as a job offer with a higher salary; or a circumstance can seem bad, such as the lingering illness of a loved one.

Jesus explained to His disciples that He always knew to respond to His Father's activity around His life. As Jesus came to the Pool of Bethesda where a host of sick people were gathered hoping to be healed, He faced two questions. First, should He heal someone on the Sabbath and bring opposition to His ministry? Second, since there was a multitude of sick people, should He heal them all or only certain ones? Ultimately, Jesus healed only one person that day, a man who had suffered for 38 years.

Later, Jesus explained how He had decided what to do (read John 5:19-20). Jesus explained that He did not come to earth to do what made sense to Him. Rather, Jesus watched to see where His Father was working and adjusted His life to become involved in that work.

Jesus assured His disciples that recognizing God at work did not involve a great deal of guesswork. Jesus knew that His Father loved Him and wanted to show Him where He was working. For example, when Jesus saw a hardened sinner so anxious to see Him that he was willing to humiliate himself publicly and climb a tree, Jesus recognized the activity of God in Zaccheus' life. Jesus knew He had to join His Father in what He was doing (Luke 19:1-10).

"The Son can do nothing of Himself, but what He sees the Father do; for whatever He does, the Son also does in like manner. For the Father loves the Son, and shows Him all things that He Himself does" (John 5:19-20).

 Explain what you will do when you face a confusing circumstance.

_____

_____

God is just as willing to reveal to you where He is at work as He was to His Son Jesus. God is working all around you. The Spirit of God will impress upon your heart when He wants you to join Him. God's Spirit may give you a holy restlessness about a certain ministry that you cannot get out of your mind. The Spirit may continually remind you of a particular work He is doing or lead someone to invite you specifically to become involved. The Spirit will give you a sense of divine peace as you adjust your life so that you are assured that God is pleased to have you join Him in His activity. The Spirit of God will also confirm His activity through Scripture and prayer.

A BUSINESSMAN WHO BECAME A MISSIONARY

Don was a Texas businessman and an active layman in his church. One day he was invited to join a singing group on a trip to the Canadian Southern Baptist Seminary. Don was offered a special opportunity to see what God was doing in Canada. The invitation was unique because the singing group consisted of professional church music directors, which Don was not. Yet Don went and had his eyes opened to what God was doing in Canada, especially at the seminary. Don was unable to forget what he experienced. God placed such a love and concern for this seminary upon Don's heart that he began to support actively and visit the school. Upon his retirement, an invitation was extended to Don to work at the seminary for two years. He and his wife Marie sold their retirement home, placed their belongings in storage, and moved to Canada. When they arrived, a local church asked him to be their pastor. The church had only 14 members and had experienced many hardships. Although Don had never been a pastor, he accepted. During Don's ministry, both the seminary and church flourished, and many people were encouraged. Don was a layperson who saw where God was at work. When Don adjusted his life to what God was doing, he experienced a wonderful time of ministry and enjoyed the thrill of being used by God.

 What circumstances are occurring around you that God may be using to speak to you? What is God saying? What response will you make?

_____

_____

Many stories could be told of people who recognized God working around them, adjusted their lives, and joined God in what He was doing. This is the pattern God has established for His people. The key is coming to know God so intimately that you are able to recognize immediately when He is working around you. When your co-worker begins to talk about spiritual things, you immediately recognize that the Spirit of God is active in your workplace. When you find yourself continually placed next to another parent at your child's school functions, you sense this is God orchestrating the events of your life so you can join His activity in this person's life. When a job offer comes the day after your church prayed, you recognize that God is opening a new door of service for you in the workplace. As you undergo difficult medical treatments for a serious illness, you are filled with a sense of peace. You realize that God is powerfully present in your life, and although He is allowing you to suffer physically, He is present and working in ways you do not understand. Pray that your eyes will be opened to see all that God is doing right around you.

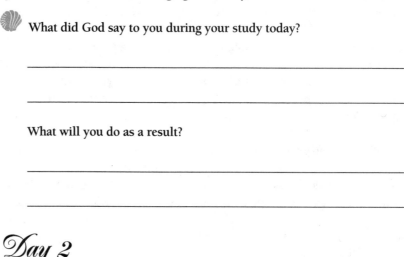 **What did God say to you during your study today?**

_____

_____

What will you do as a result?

_____

_____

Begin early this week to memorize Romans 8:28. Write it in the margin below and repeat it several times.

Day 2

CIRCUMSTANCES: CLARIFIED BY SPIRITUAL MARKERS

Can you imagine what it would be like if suddenly, tragically, you were struck with incurable amnesia? You might go to your home you had built but now, all the hours of labor, all the hopes you and your spouse shared for your dream home would be meaningless. You would greet your spouse, but all the wonderful memories of dating and marrying your sweetheart would be lost. Your hopes and fears for your children's future would no longer be important to you. How devastating it would be for you to lose your bearings for your life by forgetting all the important milestones!

The same can be true of your spiritual life. Key moments in your walk with God become spiritual markers and give a sense of direction to your life. In Joshua 4:2-3 the Israelites began entering the promised land. God had delivered them from Egypt and led them across the wilderness. He had provided water from a rock when they were thirsty and food from the sky to satisfy their hunger. Now, God performed yet another miracle by parting the Jordan River and allowing the Israelites to cross over on dry land. God commanded His people to build a monument on the banks of the Jordan (read Joshua 4:6-7). Every time an Israelite returned to this monument, they remembered that God led them into

"This may be a sign among you when your children ask in time to come, saying, 'What do these stones mean to you?' Then you shall answer them that the waters of the Jordan were cut off … And these stones shall be a memorial to the children of Israel forever" (Josh. 4:6-7).

the land and that He would sustain them. This became a wonderful teaching tool as parents reviewed with their children the great events in their walk with God.

The Bible records many times when men set up stones or built altars to signify significant encounters with God.

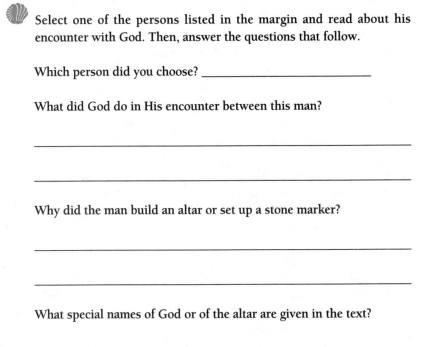 Select one of the persons listed in the margin and read about his encounter with God. Then, answer the questions that follow.

Which person did you choose? _____

What did God do in His encounter between this man?

_____

_____

Why did the man build an altar or set up a stone marker?

_____

_____

What special names of God or of the altar are given in the text?

_____

- Noah (Gen. 6-8)
- Moses (Ex. 17:8-16 or 24:1-11)
- Abram (Gen. 12:1-8 or 13:1-18)
- Isaac (Gen 26:17-25)
- Jacob (Gen. 28:10-22 and 35:1-7)
- Joshua (Josh. 3:5-4:9)
- Gideon (Judg. 6:11-24)
- Samuel (1 Sam. 7:1-13)
- David (2 Sam. 24)

SPIRITUAL MARKERS

Men in the Old Testament often built a stone marker or altar to remind them of their encounter with God. Although these people walked daily with God, there were times when God spoke so powerfully and clearly that the encounter gave direction to the rest of their lives. Places such as *Bethel* (house of God) and *Rehoboth* (room) became reminders of God's activity. Moses named an altar "The Lord is my Banner" as a reminder of a victory God granted His people. Samuel named a stone "Ebenezer" saying, "Thus far the LORD has helped us" (1 Sam. 7:12).

There were also other reminders which helped the Israelites remember what God had done. The celebration of the Passover was an annual reminder of their miraculous deliverance from Egypt. Throughout the year, an Israelite would celebrate different feasts to remember God's activity.

In the New Testament, men no longer built physical reminders of their encounters with God, but there were many "markers" which reminded them of what God had done. If you had asked Peter about his "spiritual markers," Peter might have mentioned the time Jesus walked by the fishing boat and asked him to follow, or when Jesus gave him a new name. Peter might mention walking on the water and how Jesus saved him when he began to doubt. Peter would mention the moment Jesus was transfigured before him on the mountain. Perhaps the time Jesus stooped and washed Peter's feet would be an event that affected the way Peter related to others. These spiritual markers helped Peter to see God's perspective of his life.

CHECK YOUR SPIRITUAL MARKERS

Sometimes you need to survey your spiritual markers. You will probably approach a crossroads and need to decide between two options. Often our problem is not in choosing between good and bad, but between good and best. In these times, a "good" opportunity may seem to be of God and yet may not continue to take you in the direction God has been leading you.

When I face a major decision, I review the spiritual markers of my life. A spiritual marker identifies a time of transition, decision, or direction when I clearly know that God has guided me. When I face a decision about God's direction, I rehearse those spiritual markers. I do not take the next step without reviewing the full activity of God in my life. This helps me see God's perspective on my past and present. Then I look at the options before me. I look to see which one of the options seems most consistent with what God has been doing in my life. Often one of these options will lead me in a direction about which God has already spoken. When circumstances do not align with what God is saying to me in the Bible, prayer, and the church, I continue to pray and watch until God gives me a clearer revelation of His will.

 Review your life circumstances. List some of your spiritual markers. What are some things God clearly told you ...

in your childhood? _____

_____

in your youth? _____

_____

in your adult years?_____

_____

How faithfully and completely are you obeying and implementing in your life what God has already told you?

❏ I'm doing well.
❏ There's always room for improvement.
❏ I don't have a clue.

Have you departed from God's activity? ❏ Yes ❏ No
Why do you think so?

_____

_____

Do you need to return? ❏ Yes ❏ No

What is God saying to you now?

_____

_____

How does this fit with what God has revealed to you in the past?

_____

_____

Day 3

CIRCUMSTANCES: CONFUSING APART FROM GOD

At times you may not understand the circumstances of your life. You may not have a clear word from God concerning the direction you should go. In these cases there are some basic guidelines you can follow.

WHEN CIRCUMSTANCES ARE CONFUSING

1. Settle in your mind that God forever demonstrated His love for you on the cross. That love will never change.
2. Do not try to understand what God is like based on your circumstances. Go to God and ask Him to help you see His perspective on your situation.
3. Wait on the Holy Spirit. He will take the word of God and help you understand your circumstances. Learn patience! Patience indicates that you trust that God is at work. God's timing is always best.
4. Adjust your life to God and what you see Him doing in your circumstances. Let God work in you thoroughly, so He can work through you effectively and completely.
5. If there is no clear instruction, wait and do the last thing you know God told you to do. Don't feel you have to be *doing* something all the time! When God *does* speak, do all He tells you to do.
6. Experience God working in and through you to accomplish His purposes.

 Review carefully the previous process. Circle the number by the one(s) that are easy for you. Place a check mark by the one(s) you need to work on. Will you commit to use this process the next time you face a difficult circumstance? ❑ Yes ❑ Not Sure ❑ No

Jesus said that the Holy Spirit would:

• Bring to your remembrance those spiritual markers through which God clearly spoke to you in the past. The Spirit will help you see how what He said speaks to your present circumstances, however confusing they might be.

People have called me and said, "We have prayed earnestly and even fasted, and we are convinced God wants you to come as our pastor!" Confusing? It is, especially when God had not spoken to me on the matter! The Spirit helps me see this from His perspective.

> " 'However, when He, the Spirit of truth, has come, He will guide you into all truth; for He will not speak on His own authority, but whatever He hears He will speak; and He will tell you things to come' " (John 16:13).

• Tell you of things to come (read John 16:13). When we are uncertain of a step to take, Marilynn and I pray together, and God gives His assurance to our hearts "of things to come." This was true when we went to a small church in Saskatoon. We wondered if we would ever be able to see our five children obtain a university education. With an extremely limited income, we could not afford a savings program. As we prayed, Marilynn said, "Henry, God has assured me we are doing what He wants, and that when the time comes, He will take care of our children." We believed Him and continued to serve Him without worry about tomorrow. God has indeed been faithful. All five children graduated from a university and have earned or are presently earning Masters degrees. Three have earned or are working toward doctor's degrees—all debt-free! How good and faithful God is to us! God assured us, and God brought it to pass.

🐚 **What circumstances are you currently facing that require God's perspective? Pray and ask God to reveal His perspective to you.**

🐚 **What did God say to you during your study today?**

_____

_____

What will you do as a result?

_____

_____

Day 4

CIRCUMSTANCES: EXPLAINED BY GOD

Jesus said, "I am the truth" (John 14:6). What Jesus was saying was that you can never know the truth of any situation until you have heard from God. If you try to understand your circumstances apart from your relationship to God, they will be confusing and will not seem to have any purpose. However, when you seek to understand all of your circumstances from God's vantage point, you can then appreciate His activity in even the worst of human circumstances.

Jesus is the truth in the midst of life's circumstances (read John 14:6). I have always applied this not merely to doctrine but to life. The disciples saw the storm on the Sea of Galilee as a moment when they might "perish" (Matt. 8:25). Jesus saw that they were perfectly safe because Jesus was safe, under the watchcare of His Heavenly Father. As a result, Jesus stilled the storm and then rebuked the disciples for their lack of faith. Jesus often said, "With men this is impossible, but with God all things are possible" (Matt. 19:26). For Jesus, God's presence always determined the truth of any situation.

"I am the way, the truth, and the life!" (John 14:6).

Are you in a situation where God's presence is making a difference? ❑ Yes ❑ No If yes, describe what is happening.

_____

_____

Are you afraid because you do not believe God's presence can make a difference? As a reminder of God's promise to you, write this week's memory verse three times in the margin. Then release that fear to God in prayer now.

"For all the promises of God in Him are Yes, and in Him Amen, to the glory of God through us" (2 Cor. 1:20).

"If you have faith as a mustard seed, you will say to this mountain, 'Move from here to there,' and it will move; and nothing will be impossible for you" (Matt. 17:20).

God's presence means that we should not worry. God assures us of this over and over again (Matt. 6:25,28,31-34; Phil. 4:6-7). Is God faithful and dependable when He makes a promise? God says He is (read 2 Cor. 1:20).

The moment God gives you His word, that is the reality of your situation! How simple our walk with God would be if we just believed Him! The Bible says, "And my God shall supply all your need" (Phil. 4:19). That is the truth of your circumstances. Jesus told His disciples they could move mountains (read Matt. 17:20). Do you know how you can tell if you truly believe this is the truth of your circumstances? Look around you to see how many "mountains" are being relocated! Our struggle comes when:

• God speaks the truth.
• Satan speaks the opposite.
• We have to decide who is telling the truth.

Has God spoken "truth" to you? ❑ Yes ❑ No Are you questioning or doubting the truth He has given you?

❑ I don't think so.
❑ I might be.
❑ I am.

Read the following passages in your Bible, and write beside each one the truth God is revealing in them. Ask yourself whether you are experiencing these truths in your life.

John 14:12-14— _____

Romans 8:32— _____

Romans 8:37-39—_____

Philippians 4:6-7—_____

Philippians 4:13—_____

He *is* truth! Do you believe Him?

Day 5

CIRCUMSTANCES: OPEN OR CLOSED DOORS

Many Christians today make all their decisions based on the "open door policy." That is, whenever an opportunity is presented to them, they assume they are meant to respond to it positively. Sometimes we act as if God only allows good things for our lives, so every time something comes along that appears "good," we assume it must be of God. Many people take this approach because it may seem simpler than maintaining a relationship in which God is consulted concerning each life decision. Circumstances alone cannot indicate God's will for your life.

If we were to base our decision making entirely on "open doors," we would no longer need a relationship with God; we could merely become "door watchers." Moses saw an "open door" to deliver the Israelites that cost him 40 years of herding sheep! Saul had an "open door" to offer a sacrifice, and it cost him his kingdom. Conversely, the Israelites found a "closed door" at Jericho. As they marched around the city, God brought the door and everything else down upon their enemy!

Tragically, well-meaning believers have allowed an open door to cause them to depart from God's leading. A young couple was eager to serve the Lord. A friend offered a partnership in his business. Although the couple had reservations, it seemed like an open door. The business collapsed, and the couple was saddled with a large debt. In a subsequent worship service, the couple sensed a strong call to foreign missions. As they considered applying, they realized their debt was so oppressive that they were no longer free to respond to what God had just told them. If you make a practice of automatically entering every open door, you may find your life far from the path God originally intended.

Are you facing an open door right now? ❏ Yes ❏ No If yes, what is it?

_____

How are you approaching this open door? Check all that apply.

❏ Listening for a specific word from God.
❏ Seeking counsel from other believers.
❏ Checking my spiritual markers.

ONE CLOSED DOOR LED TO MANY OPEN ONES

Early in our ministry, my wife Marilynn and I felt called to missions. We applied and were processed as missionaries. Near the end of the process, our oldest son Richard developed medical problems. The doctors suspected it could be serious. We were encouraged to wait for a year and to seek help for Richard. A door had closed. We could have assumed that God did not want us to participate in missions, but during that year, a call came from Canada. Many of the churches were weak or in decline. Numerous towns and communities had no evangelical witness. Canada was my native country, and God had given me a burden for it. Instead of going as a foreign missionary as I had supposed I would, I went as a pastor to Canada and had a glorious experience. Interestingly, once we arrived in Canada, doctors found nothing wrong with Richard's health and immediately discontinued his medication! By then we knew we were where God wanted us to be. As a result of all that I learned and experienced as a pastor in Canada, our denomination's Foreign Mission Board asked me to work with them and to travel to every mission field around the world to share with them what God had taught me during my missions experience in Canada! What appeared to be a closed door was God's way of guiding me into a ministry which far surpassed what I could ever have dreamed of doing for Him.

Christ came to John and the churches when circumstances were confusing. He promised one door would always be open—the door that leads to Christ and His guidance for your life (read Rev. 3:7-8).

Everything rests on a word from God! Do you believe Him? Are you basing your life and ministry as well as your church life on this truth? Do you practice the belief that people can never block the purposes of God? Don't let your experiences cancel this word from God. Live confidently once God has spoken.

Take inventory of your walk with God. Have you abandoned the will of God for your life because it appeared to be a closed door? Have you responded properly to closed doors in your life?

" 'He who has the key of David, He who opens and no one shuts, and shuts and no one opens': I know your works. See, I have set before you an open door, and no one can shut it" (Rev. 3:7-8).

What are some of the doors that have closed to you?

_____

How did you respond?

_____

_____

What did God say to you during your study this week?

_____

_____

What will you do as a result?

_____

_____

_____

A QUESTION OFTEN ASKED

All of my circumstances are negative. Every door of opportunity for my life seems closed. I am in the middle of a number of difficult circumstances. I have repented of every known sin. What more do I need to do? First, God may be seeking to deepen His relationship with you or to build character in you. You may be seeking "activity or assignment." God loves you. God is always active in your life. God does not waste a life. However, God never gives a large assignment to someone who is unprepared.

Second, the assignment may be waiting on your response to believe God and trust Him, even when you do not think anything is happening.

GOD SPEAKS THROUGH THE CHURCH

MEMORY VERSE

"He put all things under His feet, and gave Him to be head over all things to the church, which is His body, the fullness of Him who fills all in all" (Eph. 1:22-23).

THIS WEEK'S LESSONS

Day 1: God Speaks in the Body
Day 2: God Speaks to the Body
Day 3: God Speaks Through the Body
Day 4: God Speaks in a Unified Body
Day 5: God Speaks to Produce Christlikeness

SUMMARY OF WEEK 6

This week you will:

- determine your place in the body;
- recognize Christ as the sovereign head of the church;
- understand how God speaks through your church;
- identify areas where disharmony can harm your church; and,
- identify the common goal of the church.

A CONGREGATION THAT TESTIFIED

As a pastor, I regularly gave people an opportunity during the Sunday evening service to report what God was doing in their lives. One evening, a university student named Byron stood up nervously. He was not a church member and was unfamiliar with the customs of our church. He confessed that he was not sure if this was the "appropriate" time but that he had been earnestly seeking God and had just given his life to Christ. Byron said if the church would receive him, he would like to be baptized. I sensed that what God was saying to Byron was important enough to interrupt our service. We voted to receive him into our membership and rejoiced with him in this significant decision. Then I asked if there were others who sensed God speaking to them in a similar way. Another stood to share the decision he knew he needed to make. Many were so moved by Byron's obedience that for the next hour and a half, person after person rose to share what significant commitment they were making to Christ. I never did preach my sermon. I didn't need to. God had chosen on that evening to speak to us through Byron.

What might God do in churches if church leaders would encourage their people to testify regularly and sincerely about what God is saying to them?

Day 1

GOD SPEAKS IN THE BODY

One of the main descriptions of the local church is "the body of Christ" (read 1 Cor. 12:27 and Eph. 4:12,15-16). The biblical picture of the church has profound significance for understanding how God speaks to us and how we ought to relate to one another. Let me describe it this way.

1. God spoke to Jesus on earth and accomplished His purposes through Jesus' obedience.

2. When Jesus returned to the Father, the Father fashioned a "new body" for Christ by gathering believers together into local congregations called the church. This church is Christ's body. God adds members to the body so that each church body will be equipped to carry out His assignment.

3. Christ is the head of this new body. God guides each church through the head (Christ) and through the intimate interdependence of the members.

4. As the head, Christ directs each member to function as an integral part of the body. Together the members respond to the Head who is hearing and obeying the Father just as He did while in the flesh.

Each member must be related properly to the head and to the other members to hear all God is saying. This is God's plan for each believer. When God saves us, He immediately places us in a body of Christ—a local church—where we labor together with others on mission with Him.

This truth can be evident in a worship service. As the church body gathers to worship, the Father has a message He wants to share with His people. The Holy Spirit is present, pointing people to Jesus and guiding each member to function in the body where God placed them.

• The music leader chooses the music; people are deeply moved by God.

• Scripture is read by members; some are convicted.

• Prayer is encouraged; participants meet God during the quiet moments.

• The message is preached; people are given a clear and specific directive from God, often matching what God has been saying and doing in their lives.

• An invitation is extended; people respond to God's word and make fresh commitments to God.

 Think about the church to which God led you. God placed you with others for a purpose. How is God making a unique contribution through you to other members? On the following page, list two ways God is speaking to you through other members of your church.

"Now you are the body of Christ, and members individually" (1 Cor. 12:27).

"For the equipping of the saints for the work of ministry, for the edifying of the body of Christ … but, speaking the truth in love, may grow up in all things into Him who is the head—Christ—from whom the whole body, joined and knit together by what every joint supplies, according to the effective working by which every part does its share, causes growth of the body for the edifying of itself in love" (Eph. 4:12,15-16).

1. _____

2. _____

"Most assuredly, I say to you, he who receives whomever I send receives Me; and he who receives Me receives Him who sent Me" (John 13:20).

Jesus said that when you "receive" a Christian, you "receive" Christ (read John 13:20). This is because all of Christ is in every believer. People do not have to be Christians long before you can learn from them. Nor does it take long before they can make meaningful contributions to the church.

🐚 **Reflect on the people to whom you relate in your church. List two who have been used by God to speak to you, and identify what you learned from them.**

Person	What I learned
_____	_____
_____	_____

🐚 **What did God say to you during your study today?**

_____

_____

What will you do as a result?

_____

_____

Day 2

GOD SPEAKS TO THE BODY

When God seeks to redeem people in a community, He often begins by speaking to one church member. When this member shares his concern with his church, the church immediately senses that this is something in which God wants them to participate. The church body has been given the assignment, and it came as the head, Christ, alerted one member. When God wants to direct a church to meet the needs of college students, the local high school, or an ethnic group in the community or a foreign nation, He will speak to the body.

A CHURCH RESPONDED TO THE HEAD

While leading a conference in the Northwest, I mentioned a commitment I had made to pray for the salvation of the Armenian people. After the session, an Armenian lady came to me in tears and thanked me, telling of her family's move to America. She felt hopeless for her people back in Armenia. During the next service, I mentioned this woman and asked, "Why do you suppose God placed her in your church? Is God trying to say something to you about reaching the Armenians through you?"

The pastor, led by the Holy Spirit, asked people from other countries to come to the platform. The platform was soon filled with people. He said, "What is God saying to us? Let's pray and ask Him." Some of the dear refugees prayed in tears for their people. Finally an older man stood and prayed, "O Lord! Forgive us! We didn't know you sent these people to our church so you could minister to the nations of the world. Oh Lord, forgive us! We repent of our hardness of heart! Please Lord, if you will, use our church!" We all cried for joy. God was speaking! His people were hearing and were now willing to obey Him. Christ supplies the vision, the compassion, and the directions for the assignment. Each member responds as Christ directs him or her, and the body works together to accomplish God's purposes.

God completed all that was essential for the salvation of our world in the death, resurrection, and ascension of Jesus to His right hand. God placed Christ "far above all principality and power and might and dominion, and every name that is named, not only in this age but also in that which is to come." Then, "He put all things under His feet, and gave Him to be head over all things to the church which is His body, the fullness of Him who fills all in all" (Eph. 1:20-23).

 This week's memory verse is Ephesians 1:22-23. Write it three times in the margin as a way to place it firmly in your mind and heart.

ONE MEMBER ALERTED HIS CHURCH

Wayne, a young deaf man, came before his church under God's conviction. Wayne sensed God had an assignment for him. The church body encouraged Wayne and began praying for him. Wayne started teaching a weekly sign language class for his church and community. Then he was approached by a deaf woman, a member of a Bible study group for deaf persons which was looking for a pastor. They asked Wayne to lead them. Wayne's church body responded by voting to sponsor this new deaf church. When God spoke to one member of the body, the rest of the members responded to what they heard. Consequently they were able to participate in God's activity among the deaf community around them.

What is the Head of the church saying to you?

_____

_____

Have you shared it with the body? ❏ Yes ❏ No
Is God using you to speak to others in your church? ❏ Yes ❏ No
If yes, how?

_____

_____

Day 3

GOD SPEAKS THROUGH THE BODY

Do you remember the story of the young boy Samuel? God spoke to him during the night, but Samuel did not recognize God's voice. Samuel had not walked with God long and was unfamiliar with how God spoke to His servants. Only when he went to the older and more experienced priest, Eli, did he understand that God was speaking to him. Eli was not perfect. In fact, he was a failure as a father and was soon to be judged along with his two wicked sons. Nonetheless, Samuel grew in his understanding of how God spoke to him through the counsel of this fellow believer.

This is how your church can help you clarify what God is telling you. Although there will be a uniqueness in the way God speaks to you, there will also be similarities to how He has spoken to others in the congregation. At times, they may recognize God speaking to you before you do. At other times, they may recognize that it is not God who is speaking to you.

GOD SPEAKS THROUGH CHURCH MEMBERS

The beauty of a church is that godly people are able to witness God's activity in your life over the course of time. They see God developing your character and using you in His service. They pray for you at milestones in your life and rejoice with you in God's victories. When you come to a crossroads in your life, they are in an excellent position to help you evaluate God's direction. At times, a loving church body can offer a far more objective perspective than you could yourself.

I call interdependence a mutual, God-planned dependence on each other within the body. From the first days of the church in Jerusalem, mutual and loving interdependence were expressed. In Acts 1, Peter shared with the rest of the believers his understanding of the need to replace Judas. The church heard, prayed, and chose Matthias, agreeing that Scripture had guided them.

 Read Acts 2:42,44,46-47 in the margin and underline the phrases that indicate how the members related to each other.

In Acts 2:42,44,46-47, the bond of love in the church is obvious in the way they related to each other. What a powerful example of mutual love. Thousands who had not functioned together before were now bound intimately in love by God around a common commitment to Jesus as their Lord.

God has a purpose for each church. This may include a ministry to college students, hospital patients, or military personnel; evangelizing a particular community; supporting foreign missions; beginning new churches; or an outreach to street people. God will place members in the body who can assist the church in accomplishing its particular assignment (read Eph. 4:11-12).

As a pastor, I watched to see whom God was adding to our church to understand more fully His assignment for us.

 Look at where God has placed you in the body and what role He has given you. List below your responsibilities in your church.

_____

_____

Whatever role or task you listed above, allow Christ to teach you through the other members He has placed around you. I cannot tell you how much my life has been enriched and equipped for service by my fellow church members. It is from them that I learned about prayer, witnessing, and teaching. It is an enriching experience to place your life in the midst of the body of Christ and to let others be messengers of God to you. You will only come to understand fully what God is like as you relate to each member of the body.

"And they continued steadfastly in the apostles' doctrine and fellowship, in the breaking of bread, and in prayers. Now all who believed were together, and had all things common, ... So continuing daily with one accord in the temple, and breaking bread from house to house, they ate their food with gladness and simplicity of heart, praising God and having favor with all the people. And the Lord added to the church daily those who were being saved" (Acts 2:42,44,46-47).

"And He Himself gave some to be apostles, some prophets, some evangelists, and some pastors and teachers, for the equipping of the saints for the work of ministry, for the edifying of the body of Christ" (Eph. 4:11-12).

LEN KOSTER EQUIPPED THE BODY

After much prayer, our church sensed God directing us to start new churches. Our little church had not done that before, and we were not equipped to do so. Then God led us to invite Len Koster to join our church body. He was gifted by God in sharing his faith and starting churches. Len began to take other members with him as he led Bible studies in farmhouses or witnessed to farmers in their fields. Our members learned much about God's love for people across our land as they related to Len. Len's job was never to do all the work, but to teach and equip the members so that together we would be able to carry out God's assignment for our church.

What did God say to you during your study today?

_____

_____

What will you do as a result?

_____

_____

Day 4

GOD SPEAKS IN A UNIFIED BODY

> "As the body is one and has many members, but all the members of that one body, being many, are one body, so also is Christ....the body is not one member but many. If the foot should say, 'Because I am not a hand, I am not of the body,' is it therefore not of the body?... if they were all one member, where would the body be?" (1 Cor. 12:12,14-15,19).

Paul's letter to the Corinthians gives a vivid picture of the need for harmony in the body. During the first 11 chapters, Paul warns against such things as broken relationships and divisions in the church. In Acts 12, he paints a marvelous portrait of the church as a functioning, interrelated, and unified body (read 1 Cor. 12:12,14-15,19).

Each member differs from others but needs the others if God is to work through the body. If the whole body, Paul says, were an "eye," where would the "hearing" be? Each member is vital to the body as a whole! God speaks to the body through the "ear" so the body can "hear." God gives sight to the "eye" so the body can "see." As you relate to people in your church, remember that God purposefully places members around you who are different from you, who look at issues differently, who have different strengths and weaknesses, and who have different ministries within the church. If each member were exactly like you, your church might be seriously deficient in certain areas and unable to respond adequately to God's assignment. When each member functions as Christ has assigned, God has a healthy body through which to redeem a lost world.

Harmony—not only with Christ, but within the body—is vital to hearing from God. If barriers such as envy, anger, or not being able to forgive develop, you and your church will be hindered from hearing God's voice. Broken relationships between church members have dramatically harmed entire churches.

When Paul saw divisions beginning to form in the church in Antioch between the Gentile and Jewish Christians, he stood in a public meeting and confronted Peter. Paul understood that nothing would be more destructive to the church and its mission than to have the members divided (read Gal. 2:11-16). Yet, so subtle was the temptation of division within the church that even Peter and Barnabas allowed themselves to participate.

UNITY BROUGHT REVIVAL!

Ebenezer Baptist Church needed revival. It had many good people but was missing the manifest power of God. Two brothers, Sam and Arnold, were leaders in the church. They had been feuding for 13 years and had not spoken to each other for the last two. Their broken relationship was affecting the entire church. Then, during a week of special services, the pastor brought them together to pray. The brothers wept together over the hardness of their hearts. They confessed their sin to the church and revival began! Others confessed sin. Soon, the nightly meetings grew too large for their church building and had to be moved. Due to the crowds, the services were moved four times, until finally they met in the civic auditorium downtown. Revival swept across western Canada, into the United States and Europe. Disharmony in the body had prevented the Holy Spirit from doing a mighty work in their church!

If the "eye" is out of fellowship with other members, the whole body will be affected, sometimes very deeply. God wanted the whole church to "see" His will, but the "eye" stopped coming because of anger toward other members, and the body never saw what God had in store for it. Many church bodies operate blind, crippled, and deaf due to broken relationships. If God is going to redeem our world, it will be after He has restored His body, the church, to wholeness and effectiveness with each member functioning under the head as God has placed them in the body.

Write this week's memory verse (Eph. 1:22-23) two times in the margin below.

 How is God speaking to you through the members in your church?

_____

_____

What has God been saying...

• to you? _____

_____

• to your church? _____

_____

How are you sharing with your church what God is saying to you?
❏ Yes ❏ No

GOD SPEAKS TO PRODUCE CHRISTLIKENESS

"For whom He foreknew, He also predestined to be conformed to the image of His Son" (Rom. 8:29).

"Till we all come to the unity of the faith and of the knowledge of the Son of God, to a perfect man, to the measure of the stature of the fullness of Christ" (Eph. 4:13).

"As you therefore have received Christ Jesus the Lord, so walk in Him, rooted and built up in Him and established in the faith ... For in Him dwells all the fullness of the Godhead bodily; and you are complete in Him, who is the head of all principality and power" (Col.2:6,9).

God's goal for us is Christlikeness. He wants each of us to be like Christ who lives within us and is seeking to express His life through us. Paul repeats this theme throughout his letters (read Rom. 8:29).

What God purposes, He does! You can anticipate God's persistent and faithful activity in your life and church causing you to act, talk, love, and think like Christ (read Eph. 4:13).

Paul assured the Colossians that God's eternal purpose for every believer, and the corporate life of believers, is "Christ in you." Paul said his goal, therefore, was that "we may present every man perfect in Christ Jesus." Paul said, "Him [Christ] we preach" (Col. 1:28). (Also read Col. 2:6,9).

Because the fullness of Christ has been placed in the church, each member has access to all that God has to offer. God's plan to redeem a lost world is through the corporate life of His people. God saves people and then places them in the body of His Son, Jesus Christ. God places all His fullness in His Son. Do not underestimate the capability your church has to bring your life to Christlikeness. The elderly woman at prayer meeting may forever enrich your prayer life. That faithful deacon may change the way you handle your commitments to the Lord. That youth who boldly shares his faith at high school will challenge you to be a stronger witness. The widow who continues to give sacrificially to the Lord's work may encourage you to become a better steward. I have known people who neglected the times of corporate church life wanting only to relate to the pastor. I would always challenge them that the pastor alone could not bring them to Christlikeness. It is important that you be closely linked with a church body. Without those dear people, there will be much of Christ that you may not experience.

Do you have a personal goal, or desire to grow to be like Christ?
❏ Yes ❏ No **If yes, write it below.**

_____

_____

How are you daily letting God speak to you to conform you to the image of His Son? Check all that apply.

❏ The Bible ❏ Circumstances   ❏ The Church   ❏ Prayer

How responsive are you to the Holy Spirit who is assigned to help and enable you? Check one.

❏ Very responsive
❏ Could do better
❏ Not responsive

What evidence are you seeing of God's activity in and around you?

_____

_____

How are you joyfully and faithfully functioning in the church where God has placed you?

_____

What did God say to you during your study this week?

_____

_____

What will you do as a result?

_____

_____

A QUESTION OFTEN ASKED

You do not know my church. There is no deep level of spirituality there. I never seem to get anything out of the worship services. Should I move to a different church where I can hear God speaking to me? First, if you have a sensitive heart toward God in worship, that may be why He put you in that church. He may want to use your sensitivity to help move the church to a new level of experiencing God. Would you let God do this through you? If you leave, He cannot.

Second, you can have any kind of church, pastor, or leader you are willing to pray them to become if you are ready to let God work through you. Of course, they must also be willing to let God work in their lives. Enter into a serious commitment to pray alone and with others for your church. Be positive in your prayers for your pastor and the people!

List the key truths you have learned through this study.

_____

_____

_____

_____

_____

_____

List the commitments you have made to God during this study.

_____

_____

_____

_____

_____

Leader Guide

Each week this section will guide your group to spend sharing time together. Recommended time segments provide for one-hour sessions. Do not let this guide restrict your sharing. Freely follow the Holy Spirit's leadership. Do it yourself, or enlist a person or persons to facilitate your group sessions.

Week 1

GOD SPEAKS

REVIEW TIME (5 MINUTES)
Review this week's memory verse, Deuteronomy 8:3. Ask someone to say it and then have the group repeat it together. Ask members to share what God has said to them through this verse.

SHARING TIME (45 MINUTES)
1. Have members share ways that they have heard God speak to them in the past.
2. Ask members to explain difficulties they have had in hearing God speak to them. Discuss whether the greatest difficulty comes from actually hearing a word from God or in obeying what you know God wants you to do.
3. Ask members to identify the ways they are presenting their lives to God so He can speak to them in new or different ways.
4. Share together an experience where God spoke to each member in order to reveal something about Himself. As facilitator, share your experience first.
5. Invite members to relate an experience where God spoke to them in order to reveal His purposes.
6. Have members tell of an experience when God spoke to them in order to reveal His ways.

7. Invite members to share what kind of soil their hearts are like right now and any commitments they want to make to have hearts more receptive to a word from God. Ask if the soil of their hearts has remained the same throughout their spiritual pilgrimage or if the Holy Spirit has had to till the soil. Relate an experience where God brought the condition of your heart's soil to your attention. Then ask others to share.

PRAYER TIME (10 MINUTES)
Divide into groups of four. Pray together that you will clearly hear and understand what God says to you this week and that you will be committed to obeying God. Thank God for what He said to you this week.

Before members leave, they may want to commit themselves to contact each other during the week to see if each has kept the commitments they made to the Lord.

Week 2

GOD SPEAKS BY THE HOLY SPIRIT

REVIEW TIME (5 MINUTES)

Divide into pairs, and review your memory verse, John 16:13. Say, Share what God has been saying to you through these verses concerning your relationship to the Holy Spirit.

SHARING TIME (45 MINUTES)

1. Have members identify how the Holy Spirit has helped them clarify and accomplish God's assignment for their lives.
2. Have members tell which name and function of the Holy Spirit has been most meaningful to them recently. Look back at day 2 if needed.
3. Encourage members to share what it means to be filled with the Holy Spirit. How is one filled, and how does one remain filled?
4. Allow members to explain the kind of spiritual fruit the Spirit is presently working to produce in them.
5. Allow members to relate ways they feel they may have resisted, grieved, or quenched the Spirit.

PRAYER TIME (10 MINUTES)

Take time to divide into groups of four and pray for the following to happen.

- Members might remove anything in their lives that is preventing them from being filled by the Holy Spirit and walking intimately with Him. The group may want to pray specifically for anything that has been revealed as they worked through the material.
- Members would allow the Holy Spirit to develop specific fruit in their lives this week. Say, If the Holy Spirit has convicted you of a lack of specific fruit, pray in that area.

Week 3

GOD SPEAKS THROUGH THE BIBLE

REVIEW TIME (5 MINUTES)

Say, Review all your memory verses with a partner: Deuteronomy 8:3, John 16:13, and 2 Timothy 3:16-17. Share how God has encouraged you through these verses. After members work in pairs, lead the group in saying the memory verses.

SHARING TIME (45 MINUTES)

1. Before the session, ask a volunteer to explain the process by which the Holy Spirit speaks to us through Scripture.
2. Have members share specific ways the Holy Spirit used Scripture to speak to them. Have volunteers share their habit of personal Bible study each week. Encourage each person to establish a routine that they can follow each day.
3. Have members recall specific times and ways that Jesus used Scripture to guide His ministry; and how the early church based their actions on Scripture. Refer to day 2 if needed.
4. Discuss how you and your church can consistently seek to hear God speak to you through Scripture.
5. Have members share any commitments they made to God and His Word this week.

PRAYER TIME (10 MINUTES)

Divide into groups of four. Share an area of life the Holy Spirit has revealed that has fallen short of God's standard. Spend the remainder of the time praying for each other that each would adjust their lives to be in conformity to God's Word.

Week 4

GOD SPEAKS THROUGH PRAYER

REVIEW TIME (5 MINUTES)

Say, Divide into pairs and review all your memory verses, sharing their impact on your life. Focus particularly upon Jeremiah 33:3. Allow time for members to share all four verses they have learned in this study.

SHARING TIME (45 MINUTES)

1. Enlist someone to share the pattern in which God speaks to us through prayer.
2. Have a member explain how we can be changed through prayer. Allow members to recount times when they were changed by prayer.
3. Discuss the different kinds of responses God gives to prayer requests. How do you know if God has said yes; yes, but not yet; or no?
4. Ask for volunteers to relate what they sense God has been saying to them in their prayers lately.
5. Ask if any members feel that God is not answering prayer in their lives.
6. Discuss together possible hindrances to prayer in your family or in your church.

PRAYER TIME (10 MINUTES)

Divide into groups of three, and pray that each will hear what God says to them this week. Pray that we can accept God's answer of yes; yes, but not yet; or no for our lives.

Week 5

GOD SPEAKS THROUGH CIRCUMSTANCES

REVIEW TIME (5 MINUTES)

Say, Divide into pairs and review all your memory verses. Share what the Holy Spirit has said to you this week through these verses. Focus particularly on this week's verse, Romans 8:28.

SHARING TIME (45 MINUTES)

1. Enlist someone to give a definition of *circumstance*.
2. Remind the group what a spiritual marker is. Ask for several volunteers to share briefly some key spiritual markers of their lives.
3. Have someone explain how we should respond when circumstances are confusing.
4. Ask for someone to explain how to know whether to enter an *open door*. Ask, How should we respond to a *closed door*?
5. Invite members to explain how we can know the truth of our circumstances. See day 4 if needed.
6. Have someone share how God is speaking to them through their present circumstances—*what* God is saying and *how* God is saying it.

PRAYER TIME (10 MINUTES)

Have members divide into groups of four. Encourage them to share briefly a current circumstance in their life for which they need prayer. Pray within the small groups for each member according to the request.

Week 6

GOD SPEAKS THROUGH THE CHURCH

REVIEW TIME (10 MINUTES)

Say, Repeat with me this week's memory verse, Ephesians 1:22-23. Repeat it as a group. Divide into pairs, and review your memory verses for the six weeks. Ask members to share what God has said to you through the memory verses.

SHARING TIME (35 MINUTES)

1. Discuss whether the members feel their church is more of a religious organization or the body of Christ.
2. Share how Christ helps a church know the will of God. See day 1 if needed.
3. Have the members testify how other members of their church helped them to know the will of God.
4. Say, Take a personal spiritual inventory. How are you growing toward Christlikeness? Share where you need help from others.
5. Have members share what part of the body God has placed them in and how He is presently using them to build up the body.

PRAYER TIME (5 MINUTES)

Divide into groups of four and pray for:
• Knowing your place in the body of Christ.
• Commitment to pray for each other and the commitments you have made during this study.
• Commitment to function in the body where God put you for the common good of all.

REFLECTION (5 MINUTES)

Discuss briefly the value of this study. Allow members to share one or two sentences about what God has done in their lives during the past six weeks.

Ask, What do you sense that God wants you to do next to continue the process of hearing and understanding His word to you? Consider these ideas.

• Continue meeting regularly as a group for encouragement and prayer.
• Study *Experiencing God: Knowing and Doing the Will of God* or *The Mind of Christ*. These 13-week courses will take you into a much deeper study. These resources may be purchased by writing the Customer Service Center; 127 Ninth Avenue, North; Nashville, TN 37234; calling 1-800-458-2772; faxing (615) 251-5933; ordering online at *www.lifeway.com*; emailing *customerservice@lifeway.com*; or visiting a LifeWay Christian Store.

CHRISTIAN GROWTH STUDY PLAN

Preparing Christians to Serve

In the **Christian Growth Study Plan (formerly Church Study Course)**, this book *When God Speaks* is a resource for course credit in the subject area Ministry of the Christian Growth category of diploma plans. To receive credit, read the book, complete the learning activities, show your work to your pastor, a staff member or church leader, then complete the following information. This page may be duplicated. Send the completed page to:

Christian Growth Study Plan
127 Ninth Avenue, North, MSN 117
Nashville, TN 37234-0117
FAX: (615)251-5067

For information about the Christian Growth Study Plan, refer to the current Christian Growth Study Plan Catalog. Your church office may have a copy. If not, request a free copy from the Christian Growth Study Plan office (615/251-2525).

When God Speaks
CG-0125

PARTICIPANT INFORMATION

Social Security Number — Personal CGSP Number* — Date of Birth

Name (First, MI, Last) ☐ Mr. ☐ Miss ☐ Mrs. ☐   Home Phone

Address (Street, Route, or P.O. Box) | City, State | Zip Code

CHURCH INFORMATION

Church Name

Address (Street, Route, or P. O. Box) | City, State | Zip Code

CHANGE REQUEST ONLY

☐ Former Name

☐ Former Address | City, State | Zip Code

☐ Former Church | Zip Code

Signature of Pastor, Conference Leader, or Other Church Leader | Date

*New participants are requested but not required to give SS# and date of birth. Existing participants, please give CGSP# when using SS# for the first time. Thereafter, only one ID# is required. Mail to: Christian Growth Study Plan, 127 Ninth Ave., North, MSN 117, Nashville, TN 37234-0117. Fax: (615)251-5067

If you want to learn more about knowing and doing the will of God, check out
Experiencing God!

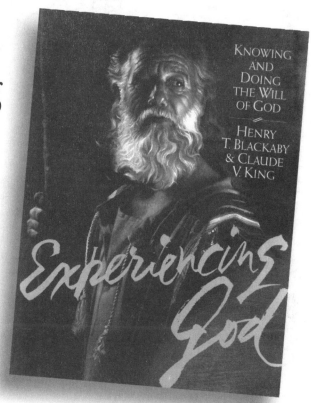

Experiencing God: Knowing and Doing the Will of God, by Henry T. Blackaby and Claude V. King, is a course in applied, living theology. It's a daily step-by-step guide through the unfolding drama of His plan. His plan for your life. His plan for your church. God's plan for the ages.

Instead of struggling to find some rhyme or reason to your own life's direction, you'll learn how to see your significance in light of God's overarching purposes for His kingdom. And His purposes alone.

You'll learn to pattern your walk with God after the example set by the great men and women of the Bible—people who heard God's call, responded in simple faith and obedience, and altered the history of entire nations by losing themselves in the eternal purposes of God.

If you want wisdom that speaks louder than words, perspective that goes beyond your four walls, and a life that lives what you say you believe, you'll have to experience it for yourself ...with *Experiencing God*. (ISBN 0-8054-9954-7)

To obtain more information or to place an order, contact Customer Service Center, MSN 113; 127 Ninth Avenue, North; Nashville, TN 37234-0113; fax (615) 251-5933; email customerservice@lifeway.com; or order online at www.lifeway.com.

Try our other
Everyday Discipleship courses!

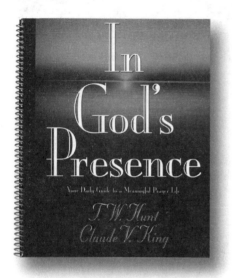
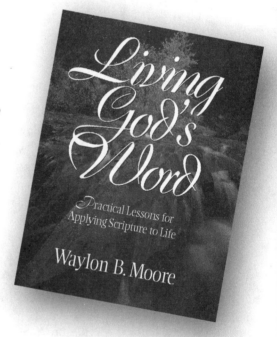